THIS BOOK
BELONGS TO

....

....

Author's Afterthoughts

With so many books out there to choose from, I want to thank you for choosing this one and taking precious time out of your life to buy and read my work. Readers like you are the reason I take such passion in creating these books.

It is with gratitude and humility that I express how honored I am to become a part of your life and I hope that you take the same pleasure in reading this book as I did in writing it.

Can I ask one small favour? I ask that you write an honest and open review on Amazon of what you thought of the book. This will help other readers make an informed choice on whether to buy this book.

My sincerest thanks.

©COPYRIGHT 2024

The content contained within this book may not be reproduced, duplicated, or transmitted without direct written permission from the author or the publisher. Under no circumstances will any blame or legal responsibility be held against the publisher, or author, for any damages, reparation, or monetary loss due to the information contained within this book. Either directly or indirectly.

Legal Notice:
This book is copyright protected. This book is only for personal use. You cannot amend, distribute, sell, use, quote, or paraphrase any part, or the content within this book, without the consent of the author or publisher.

Disclaimer Notice:
Please note the information contained within this document is for educational and entertainment purposes only. All effort has been executed to present accurate, up-to-date, and reliable, complete information. No warranties of any kind are declared or implied. Readers acknowledge that the author is not engaging in the rendering of legal, financial, medical, or professional advice. The content within this book has been derived from various sources. Please consult a licensed professional before attempting any techniques outlined in this book. By reading this document, the reader agrees that under no circumstances is the author responsible for any losses, direct or indirect, which are incurred as a result of the use of the information contained within this document, including, but not limited to — errors, omissions, or inaccuracies.

Table of Contents

Chapter I — 8
Chapter II — 17
Chapter III — 25
Chapter IV — 28
Chapter V: — 36
Chapter VI — 41
Chapter VII — 47
Chapter VIII — 49
Chapter IX — 80
Chapter X — 96
Chapter XI — 98
Chapter XII — 104
Chapter XIV — 111
Chapter XV: — 118
Chapter XVI: — 124
Chapter XVII — 131
Chapter XVIII: — 134
Chapter XIX — 139

HOW TO START YOUR EPIC ONLINE BUSINESS

Begin your journey by taking all the right steps to ensure your venture a guaranteed success!

Introduction

Thank you for downloading this guide, and more importantly, Congratulations!

Starting out as a digital entrepreneur running an online business is an exciting new journey.

There's no better time in history to own an online business. Despite what you may hear in the media, we are living in the golden age of unlimited income and wealth. With the internet and technology there are vast opportunities out there that are ripe with opportunity and potential for extreme online business growth at a never-before-seen scale of abundance.

The catch is - the direction is wide open, and there is not just one single way to get to your destination.

There are many directions, and it is extremely easy to get side tracked and knocked off your path to complete each level to success.

This is guide is designed to help you navigate the many common curves, pitfalls and strategies to help you avoid common distractions like 'Shiny Object Syndrome' and other situations you'll encounter. It will help to keep you on track and focused towards your goal of making a profitable and sizeable income with your online business.

Whenever you start a new business as an entrepreneur; whether you're a freelancer, copywriter, content creator, website developer, blogger, SEO consultant, social media specialist, ecommerce owner, etc... there are many ways to go about it.

There are independent websites and specialized businesses where you can find a new or currently operating online business through specific communities on the web or;

You can take the matter into your own hands. And create your own from scratch. Some people prefer to work hard and take care of every little detail themselves.
This involves multiple steps and fortunately, it doesn't have to be this way!
Getting the word out about your online business across the globe is the most important factor to focus on.

So, now let's get started!

Regardless of what route you choose, your online business begins by choosing a proper niche, being organized, having self-discipline, developing a laser focus, persistence, skills, and turning your ideas into reality!

You Have Skills: Now Let's Make Some Real Money from Them

Chapter I

How to Build a Winning Online Brand

Building an online brand can be tricky business.

Fact. People buy from people and businesses they like and trust. They don't buy the product first hand.

Ask yourself, how can you make your products or services appealing and authentic to stand out amongst the competition? What do you think will make people want to purchase from your business over another?

When you make random purchases yourself online is it due to the look, the website design, the hype behind it, the marketing materials, the mission, or perhaps because the company you're buying from makes an incredible product, offers money back guarantees and provides a wonderful service?
Some brands attract millions of viewers and have an incredible customer loyalty base simply because they are hyped up by certain celebrities or influencers who promote them.

Nowadays with the expanse of the Internet anyone can offer and build a successful online 'brand' seemingly overnight.

Whether you have a personal brand or commercial one you'll find that building a brand, although tons of fun, is definitely not a straight and narrow path.

Every brand and business after all is different and unique. What works for one brand, won't necessarily work for the next. And in order to remain relevant over the long term, you have to constantly be looking for ways to adapt and move with the times.

To increase exposure, attracting a loyal fan base is the first step. You will draw in more customers with these 5 digital marketing tips and strategies just about any online brand can use:

1. **Don't get overly attached to any one platform**.

Remember that the Internet and social media is constantly in flux.

You must accept the fact that what works today may not work tomorrow. One day you may see your Pinterest traffic flying through the roof and the next day Pinterest might change its algorithm and all your hard-earned traffic has gone down the tubes. Same thing with Google.

Worse yet, you may spend years investing in building your presence on a social media platform only for that platform to possibly become irrelevant, or obsolete altogether.

This is what makes the world of digital marketing so interesting. It's an ever-changing world of testing, altering, adapting and never becoming too reliant upon any one method.

So, don't get your knickers all in a bunch if what worked perfectly one day all of a sudden goes to pot the next. The moment these tactics no longer work, stop and switch gears and look for another solution.

The good news is there will always be one.

Tip 2:

2. **Be prepared to use today's growth hacks to your advantage.**

The internet is not exactly like the IRS tax codes. There is no formal rule book.

When it comes to building a winning brand and business online, you have to understand that you are competing with some serious digital marketers who will do whatever it takes in order to succeed.

These include Twitter and Instagram bots, folks running Live Facebook videos 24/7, cheesy YouTube get rich now "vlogger" ads, that use clickbait headlines, buy massive email lists, and even utilize black hat SEO tactics. You name it!

As a reputable brand and online business, you have to make the choice where you want to draw the line and how you want to present yourself.

Of course, it's important to promote yourself and get traffic, make sales and make money. That's what you're in business for.

But you always want to go about it in an ethical way.

Anyone looking to build a brand and business online needs to educate themselves on how the Internet actually works rather than on how you wish it would work.

And part of that education process means knowing all the different ways to gain exposure, sell products, acquire email addresses, build sales funnels, promote your business and gain more traffic the right way.

Because some marketers out there will do anything to try to get you to sell you these methods which could put you and your valuable reputation at risk.

Don't fall for it. Sometimes slow and steady wins the golden egg.

Tip 3:

3. **Invest heavily in focused methods that drive the most results for your brand.**

So many companies get caught in the vicious cycle of "trying to be everywhere at once."

This is a trap and a mistake. Being a Jack or Jill of all trades can lead you down the road to being master of 'none'.

It's not necessary for you to spend hours upon hours being on every single social media platform out there it it's not working for you.

This will be a huge waste of time, money and effort.

If you're paying someone to promote you on LinkedIn and you're getting no traffic, no conversions, no clicks and no engagement from that particular platform there's really no point.

The key is not to invest money or time in areas where your audience is not.

On the other hand, if your Facebook ads are returning an interest this is an investment you can depend on. Put your energy into mastering that platform and method and ditch the rest.

The secret is knowing who your audience is, what they're interested in and where they visit.

Unless you're a Fortune 500 company with a massive advertising budget, it's actually far more effective to invest in a small handful of initiatives that have been proven to work for your business.

So, stop trying to be on Twitter, Instagram, Tumblr, Tik Tok, Facebook, Reddit, Pinterest, and LinkedIn all at the same time.

Tip 4:

4. **Pay Attention to the Analytics**

One of the greatest advantages the Internet has provided businesses is the ability to acquire amazing insights and data in terms of your audience which helps your online business efforts incredibly.

Sure, it's a great boost to the ego if you have 100K likes and followers on Instagram but are you making any money from it?

Are these followers actually going on to your website and making purchases? Or are these simply 'vanity' likes.

If you find that people are just looking at your pretty pictures and your posts just for the heck of it, what use are your marketing initiatives if you're pouring money and time into these efforts but have no real outcome for success.

On the flip side, if you can determine that 10% of these likes are actually converting into sales, then perhaps it is worth it and you can expand your achievements from there.

Setting arbitrary goals without firmly defining how those goals are going to move your brand and business to the next level is a complete waste of time, money, and resources.

So, before you determine whether you should put more money towards a certain social media platform to promote your online business, you should question whether those initiatives are truly going to move the needle for your business in the first place.

Tip 5:

5. **Consistency is more important than anything else.**

The Internet moves fast and there's a ton of noise.

There's an expression 'A River cuts through a rock not because of its power but its persistence'.

You can also switch that word to consistency. At any single moment, there is such an unfathomable amount of content and noise for people to pay attention to, that brands have to remember the one thing that's going to make a difference over the long term.

The power of consistency will take your online business to new heights.

Remember, you've got to be in it for the long haul. Just like any great marriage or relationship, it's a marathon not a race, and the one who sticks with their business and brand through the hard times wins.

You must show you have the power of long-lasting value, be credible, be authentic and transparent.

Don't throw in the towel at every frustration or bump in the road.

And that's the best way to build your winning brand!

Chapter II

The Huge Benefits of Outsourcing

The benefits of outsourcing are substantial. Running any online business all by yourself is a mighty tall task.

If you're like me, you have a hundred little things that are on your to-do list that keep interfering with the larger tasks.

It's easy to get overwhelmed when you throw all the marketing minutiae on top of what you already need to do to keep things running smoothly.

This is where hiring a freelancer to **outsource your work can literally save you from going insane.**

In fact, you may be surprised to learn that most businesses rely on outsourcing to get things done so they can continue to work on growing their businesses and focus more on the core.

Your reasons may be different. If you're just starting out you may find that you really don't want to spend 2 hours of research preoccupied with which WordPress plugins you should download, which logo to choose, or which theme to import.

Let's face it this can easily lead to 'shiny ball syndrome' and take you off your course big time.

Or say you're a consultant and you have several things you have to do for a client, but you only have X amount of time in a day to handle billing and administrative tasks.

These tasks can all be outsourced to save you precious resources, and most importantly your sanity.

A lot of tasks are just plain laborious, tedious, and only hold you back from focusing on more pressing matters such as the larger picture.

Outsourcing also doesn't mean that you have to be completely hands-off.

When running your own online business you do have to be on top of things and involved in many if not all of the little decisions even if someone else is actually implementing them.

This is where scheduling tools like Monday.com, Asana, Trello and others can keep everything you're managing all in one place and help you and your team stay on top of things and organized.

Costs of Outsourcing

Of course, if you're just starting a business, I'm sure one of your first concerns is the cost of outsourcing.

Undoubtedly you have to pay for quality work.

But you have to put things into perspective. Doesn't it make sense to pay someone say $17 per hour to post on social media for you when realistically it would take 6 hours out of your day to create posts, descriptions, videos, hashtags and more; potentially costing you a lot more for each hour of your time?

If you can be doing your work for the amount you charge, take care of your clients and get all other necessary tasks done then it's a win/win situation for all.

Risks to Outsourcing for your Online Business

As in life, there are risks to anything.

You can risk hiring someone who does a lousy job and you have to wind up doing the whole project over, or someone who doesn't complete the job on time, or someone who makes your brand look less than what you expect.

But I say the benefits outweigh the risks by far.

Some entrepreneurs and marketers are concerned they'll get low quality work if they outsource.

What I've discovered and many other business owners have as well is that you can actually improve the quality of work if you outsource.

Let's say you need to create an animated video for a new company. You can try and attempt it yourself, do all kinds of research that takes up an entire day, look up all kinds of programs and techniques before finally attempting it.

Or you can find someone right away who specializes in just that, that comes with great reviews, tons of experience, samples and can get it done in 24 hours. Makes sense right?

If you outsource the work, the quality will be a million times better than the quality you'd get if you'd tried to do it yourself. And you won't feel like drowning yourself in a bottle of wine at the end of the day.

I know that as an entrepreneur we can get 'stuck' on being perfect and trying to control everything.

But this can seriously paralyze you and keep you from the big picture of what you need to do to grow your business.

You don't always need perfection when it comes to marketing. **Sometimes you just need to get it done!**

And the good thing is, freelance online platforms nowadays have made sure that their creators have to be accountable in the form of receiving reviews. After all, no one wants a poor review.

Here's some ways freelancers and outsourcing can make your life so much easier:

Outsourcing content marketing

Do you really have 4 -8 hours a day to write a blog post? I know I don't! That eats up a tremendous amount of time.

Multiply that by 4-12 blog posts per month, plus uploading, optimizing for SEO, editing, adding relevant links, images, videos, affiliate links, that's a serious amount of time!

"That's why over 64% of marketers outsource their content writing nowadays. Blogs deliver an average of **434% more indexed webpages and 97% more in-**links (for SEO)

Thankfully, while content is becoming increasingly important for Marketing teams – marketers now spend, on average, 25% of their total budget on content – it's also something that can be easily outsourced to agencies and consultants". – According to Oursocialtimes.com

Outsourcing a content writer or professional blogger can definitely improve your efficiency.

You as an independent business owner cannot run your business adequately unless you have superhuman powers or outsource content marketing tasks.

Here's some examples of what you can outsource:

- Creating offsite content that links back to your website and blog
- Interviewing sources
- Finding statistics to add
- Blogger outreach
- Repurposing content, using a variety of mediums such as infographics, videos, slideshows and webinars
- Creating and managing your editorial calendar
- Establishing deadlines for content
- Building spreadsheets for your editorial calendar
- Backing up content
- Finding and editing photos
- Converting files
- Working on increasing post engagement
- Keeping track of your budget
- Ensuring all content is mobile-friendly

As you can see all of this will take major time and effort.

Outsourcing Social Media Marketing is a Must

In my opinion, social media marketing is something you **absolutely need to outsource!**

We've touched upon the enormous amount of time it takes to curate relevant articles you want to share with your audience and that match up to your companies' vision!

Not only that, you have to add visuals as well as comment and respond to people 24/7/365.

Outsourcing this task is an instant way to free up several hours a week!

Outsourcing SEO

Outsourcing SEO can be a little different. You want to make sure the person you assign to this has a proven track record of managing accounts, growing their organic rankings and knows what they're doing.

Many virtual assistants can help with basic functions of on-page SEO like creating meta tags, headers and site maps, some more complex logistics should be left to someone who knows the ins and outs of technical SEO well.

Not to mention deciphering website analytics, insights and what type of content is getting the most traffic for you.

With all the many detailed technical, creative, analytical and planning aspects that go into an online business, you'd certainly be wise to utilize the experience and talent of the many [freelance outsourcers](#) out there.

Once you start, you'll find it hard to imagine doing things any other way. It will make a world of difference for you in terms of cost savings, efficiency and competitive advantage.

A Special Note About Freelancers

I believe sometimes when people hear the word "Freelancer," they often think of someone who does something part time, in between their 'real' job for a low wage.

I think it gives one the perception of doing easy work they could get 'anyone for' at a low-cost value - hence they are willing to try and low ball you for the lowest amount possible.

Well, just remember you get what you pay for.

It is important for people to understand that the freelancing world isn't about "temporary" work anymore.

Independent freelance consultants and entrepreneurs are highly skilled, experienced, professional and very engaged with the jobs they have to perform.

Hold yourself, people who outsource for you, and your business in high esteem and don't cut corners. It will only bite you in the long run.

Chapter III

Buh - Bye 9-6! - The Popularity of Entrepreneurship and Freelancing

Consider the trifecta combination of factors; the economic recession from getting hit head on with the novel Covid-19 Virus - a desire for flexibility, as well as the continuous development of technology has made it more possible for people to make momentous gains while working from home and not only that! But from anywhere on the planet (practically speaking).

Not only have so many brick and mortar shops made the transition to an all-online business, but individuals have been starting businesses online in record numbers.

Even with little to no money, it's not only a possibility but a reality.

All of my projects are completed from home and delivered to clients all over the world. With little to no overhead.

As long as you have an internet connection and a laptop that works you can make money. And heaps of it.

Some Facts About the Remote Job Market

The remote job market is showing unprecedented growth. It's grown by over 500% according to Paychex. And that was way back in 2014! Between start-ups, Millennials, Gen Z, and technology there is no shortage of online business opportunities and jobs online.

In fact, if you're thinking about entering the content marketing industry, it has been forecasted to be a **$400 plus billion** dollar industry, according to The Content Marketing Institute.

In 2014 it was $196 Billion and in 2021 it's due to double.

The beauty of the internet is you can literally launch a business and make money online with little to no capital.

Compare that to a physical store with crushing overhead, overblown taxes, employee benefits, unemployment payments, vendor costs, rising insurance rates, etc, etc. Headache upon headache.

Take for example the huge shift in the amount of content writers need in all industries right now. There's actually a shortage of content out there. Remote writers and people who are able to write for others while making their own schedules and work from home.

And this is only one example of online work that's available now.

According to Paychex - "At the moment, there are around 53 million entrepreneurs working in the United States.

Out of them all, 14.3 million are people who have full-time jobs, but also perform entrepreneurial tasks when time allows it – they are also known as "moonlighters".

Another 9.3 million people do freelance work in combination with part-time jobs. The remaining people are working as full-time entrepreneurs going from project to project. By 2021, it is estimated that over 60% of the workforce available in America will be pursuing independent work".

According to NPR.org - It literally took a global pandemic to force the move to remote work for a third of Americans.

Chapter IV

Are You Cut Out for Entrepreneurship?

With entrepreneurship and starting an online business you still have to weigh out the pros vs cons. I frankly believe there are more pros to being an entrepreneur but you must decide for yourself, your family, your personality and your personal situation.

Let's mention just a few of the plus sides of running your own online business, shall we?

Pros of Being an Entrepreneur
- The ability to make your own schedule (great work/life balance)
- Not having to commute everyday
- Not spending money on gas
- Not having to spend money on work 'attire'
- Not spending thousands of dollars on daycare or pet care for that matter!
- Being able to easily make time for necessary appointments
- Taking yoga/snack/coffee breaks anytime
- Working at night or whenever you feel like it
- Setting your own rates
- Having a sense of ownership of your career
- UNLIMITED earning potential

- Getting to pursue your own passions not someone else's dreams
- No office politics and back-stabbing
- Being able to be selective with whom you work with and for

Some 'Cons' of Entrepreneurship to Consider

- Lack of company provided health benefits (although many companies are forcing US workers these days to provide their own health benefits - and some freelance providers like Fiverr are teaming up with insurance companies to provide benefits for entrepreneurs.
- Feeling isolated - if you're the type of person who always needs to be around people this may not be for you
- Juggling multiple clients - You must be able to focused and organized
- Hustling for new gigs - In the beginning you will have to learn to promote yourself
- Running every business aspect (sales and marketing, invoicing, signing contracts, troubleshooting technology, keeping track of tax deductible business expenses, making estimated tax payments, etc. – According to Monster.com

Is Your Personality Suited for Entrepreneurship?

It's a known fact that working from home, as appealing as it may sound at times for some, can become maybe a little bit lonely at times.

Will you miss the office schmoozing? The camaraderie of co-workers, office get togethers, and daily chit chat?

Of course, as an entrepreneur you are not completely isolated! You will have plenty of interactions with clients, other people in your business, vendors etc. You're not stuck on a deserted island completely cut off from all social contact!

For me, I found it to be the perfect situation! I can get all my work done as needed without any distractions. No phones ringing, no office gossip, nonsense I don't want to hear about distracting me, being as creative as I want, and making my own unlimited income. It's awesome!

But not everyone is like this and some people need to have others around them at all times, I get it.

There are other types of freelancing jobs and online businesses you can have where you are around people mind you, but we're speaking specifically of remote digital work themes in this guide in particular.

Remote Work Platforms

There are numerous numbers of platforms that connect freelance workers with multinational organizations or even small local businesses.

A primary example of this type of business is Upwork, Fiverr, and a new one called Freeup Freelancers.com.

Upwork is a company which manages to connect 3.6 million organizations with over 9 million entrepreneurs from all around the world (180 countries to be more precise).

This platform allows large corporations to hire people when the need for a full-time employer isn't justified and the need for cost control is very important.

A lot of small businesses profit from this service as well, especially when they require help with their finances, marketing strategies or even a product launch.

This type of platform is ok to start with if you need to build up a portfolio.

The downside is that Upwork takes a percentage of the entrepreneur's rate. So, if you increase your hourly rate it makes it harder to compete with others out there who are bidding for the same job forcing you to drive your price down in order to get jobs if you are just starting out.

Another thing is that if you don't consistently bid on jobs they move your profile to 'hidden' making it impossible for potential companies to find you because they can't see you unless you pay Upwork a fee to be seen!

I understand Upwork needs to make money but this isn't a fair practice in my opinion.

I prefer a job board such as Fiverr or Pro Blogger (if you're a freelance writer) or any one of the 100 other sites I list on my blog if you're seeking professional writing/blogging work. This popular list features over 100+ sites that pay writers anywhere from $50 - $2,000 per post.

Fiverr is a source I use and recommend because on this platform you can apply for no fee, and set up a 'gig' which lists and describes your services.

There are no upfront costs to do business on Fiverr. It's a good place to start even if you have limited experience. If you have an idea and a creative mind and a portfolio with some reviews you'll do even better.

Some entrepreneurs I know have started their own businesses on Fiverr making upwards of 5 - 6 figures a year.

These freelancers provide high quality services to companies and other entrepreneurs, and maintain consistent 5-star reviews.

The only costs you have is if you choose to invest in tools to improve your creation of products and services such as software or materials.

Opportunities for digital freelancing gigs on Fiverr in particular are many. However, keep in mind, depending on your niche, you could be in for some stiff competition. But! This can be a good thing because that means the niche makes MONEY!

And you can differentiate yourself from the rest of the herd as long as you provide top quality work consistently along with excellent customer service.

As an entrepreneur on Fiverr or Fiverr Pro which showcases some of the upper elite and higher-level freelancing talent, you can specialize in a certain area of expertise. This is an excellent way in which you would hold an advantage over others and build up a 'top rated' rating fast.

This way, you can literally start an online business with virtually no money. Here are just some of the many services you can offer on Fiverr:

- Copywriting/Content Writing
- Virtual Administrative services
- Graphic Design
- Website Development
- Sales Copy
- Editing/Proofreading
- Email Templates/Funnels
- WordPress Help
- SEO services
- Pinterest Specialist
- Social Media Manager

- PowerPoint/MS Office
- Digital drawings
- Logos/Business Cards/ Resume Design
- Video Creation/Editing
- Voice Overs! The list goes on….

Fun Hobbies Can Turn into an Online Business

Think about what you enjoy doing. If whatever you do feels like work then you will not want to continue doing it. Part of being an entrepreneur and starting your own business is enjoying and wanting to expand upon what you already do, or have a talent for, and maintaining a real passion for it. Tailor your work around this idea.

Make certain that you're charging a fair and competitive price for your gigs so that it's something that will benefit both you and your clients.

You may have to charge less in the beginning but Fiverr also offers 'tiers' which allows you to charge more when you offer more options.

There's also add-on services such as rush delivery, revision options and more, so what may sound like a $5 gig can really amount to much more. There's also the option of receiving tips from your satisficed clients.

We'll talk more about how to get paid as an online business in further detail in the later chapters.

And don't worry, many entrepreneurs start out with little to no credibility in the industry. It might take some time to build a solid reputation for yourself. In particular, growing your business might be a slow process when you join communities such as Fiverr or Upwork.

On these platforms you stand a chance of building a better reputation based on customer reviews over time.

If your services are truly superior, as mentioned above you can move onto the '[Fiverr Pro](#)' echelon group of entrepreneurs who have proven themselves to be the best of the best in their niche.

These professionals are able to charge significantly more for their services.

Remember Fiverr is just one platform to test the waters and start an online business.

Perhaps utilizing this platform you can be one of the many who runs a $100K business.

Chapter V:

Identify Your Marketable Skills and Turn Them into Hot Profits

The first step toward starting a successful career as an online business owner is to identify the nature and niche of your business. In other words, what are you good at? What are you dying to share or offer your skills for?

What can you see yourself doing for a long time? And how can you monetize your expertise and turn it into a viable online business?

Define Your Business and Your Personal Brand

As an entrepreneur, you should be responsible for every aspect of your online business. In essence, you are your own business!

It is always very strange when you see businesses that are obviously run by a single person, yet they hide behind a fake company website and use expressions such as "One of our representatives will assist you shortly" just to give off the impression that they are a bigger firm.

To be completely blunt, people aren't stupid, especially those who are accustomed to buying services from entrepreneurs. Don't try to lie about the scale of your operation.
Instead, take pride in the fact that you are doing this by yourself!

Why would you hide behind an obviously fake corporate name when you can proudly endorse your own personal brand?

Even if you choose to select a name for your business (as opposed to using your actual given name), you can still give the audience a sense of bespoke authenticity and personality, if you use the right approach to branding.

Being a "solo show" is not a limitation, and it shouldn't be seen as a negative thing. You are not competing with huge Fortune 500 companies.
Instead, you are offering an alternative. For some people, hiring an entrepreneur is a big perk. Many customers look for a "face-to-face" experience.

They want to deal with a real person who does real work, not with a faceless big company rep who is going to direct them to the next call center when they need some customer support.

Show your customers that you are doing this on your own, because your goal is to give clients a dedicated, personal service. Show them that you are proud of your work, so much so that you are willing to associate your name and image to it.

Be sure to really put your own personality into your personal brand, and be transparent about the scope of your business.

If customers ask you about your process, don't be wary about sharing more details and walk them through how you do things.

Turning Your Skills into a Marketable Online Business.

One of the most difficult things to do being an entrepreneur or starting an online business, is to determine how to actually make money from it.

Although platforms like Fiverr as I mentioned make it very easy to structure prices, it is definitely possible to use different approaches.

Vital Skills to Run an Online Business

One of the most effective skills and solutions you need to have for your online business is excellent communication.

When a potential customer fills out an inquiry or approaches you about a service, don't try to jump on a sale immediately.

Instead, take your time to thoroughly make sure that you can fulfill the customer's request. Ask questions and get as many details as you can from the prospect customers.

This way, you will be able to get a better perspective on the amount of work to be done, thus charging your customer accordingly.

It is very important to lay all the cards on the table. This means that you should be completely transparent about your fees.

You should also be very clear about other aspects of your offering.

There should be no confusion concerning delivery times, revision policies and the scope of the project in general.

If you work out all the kinks in advance you can avoid many issues when working on the project and dealing with the client.

Getting everything worked out in the beginning also means that you can decrease the risk of wrongful claims or exploitation.

Some buyers might want more services than what was previously agreed, so it is very important to prevent them from taking advantage of you.

A good way to make sure everything is clear and upfront is to have all the appropriate and necessary legal agreements or contracts already in place.

Another valuable skill and effective form of communication if you already have a website, is to have a detailed form.

I use WordPress forms on my site to collect vital client information beforehand.
I like them because they are inexpensive and you can customize them anyway you like using different questions of your choice. This gives you the option to collect leads as well as automatically add them to your email list.

Having everything in writing about every aspect of a project is the best way to communicate that you are a professional and can help avoid you being taken for a ride!

Chapter VI

The Most Profitable Online Businesses

Okay! So, you have your mind set on creating your own online business but where exactly do you begin?

There are so many resources out there and so much information. You are overwhelmed. You know you need to do a lot of research creating the different steps that go into making your online business a success.

There are a lot of moving parts and the process needed to build a business online is fairly similar to building an actual brick and mortar business.

Key Things to Consider

When choosing to start your business online you will need to decide on certain things right away;

1) How will you decide on a design for your website?
2) Will you design it yourself or will you outsource a website design company?
3) You will need a logo and a brand name
4) You will need content in the form of copywriting, product lists, images, pricing and more.
5) You will need to implement the proper legal attributes such as disclosures, privacy information, copyright protection and disclaimers.
6) You will need to get traffic to your website via SEO, PPC ads, Facebook ads and advertising.
7) You will need someone to handle social media marketing for you.
8) You will need to develop an email list to collect customer information and continuous communication.
9) You will need someone to manage reviews for you.
10) You will need to have a website developer on hand to help you with certain problems and technical issues with the website.

This is why you need dependable help (in the form of outsourcing) and a solid strategy towards building your successful online business rather than one that leads you nowhere.

Create a Thriving Online Presence

The internet has greatly diversified the way we do our business transactions in the modern world. Many people actually use the internet for self-branding also known as personal branding.

This is enabled through the use of social media and blogging. A website is the one sure-fire way for building a successful brand online and making money along the way.

If you work online or your business has a site already hosted on the internet, you are headed in the right direction with regards to growing your business online and creating a great income stream.

This is the information age and investing in an online business is a desirable venture for you. It is not very costly and in the process, you will get to learn from the many benefits.

My digital marketing blog, Socialbuzzhive teaches people the strategies they need to grow their presence online and work remotely.

Whatever you do, having an online business means that a thriving online presence is crucial.

To quote Bill Gates "If your business is not on the internet, then your business will be out of business."

Some people have been successful at building their own businesses without anyone's help. However, if you were to talk to one of these successful business owners, you would find they spent years struggling to make their business a success.

This doesn't have to be the case! But if you don't take advantage of the experience of people who have already been through the ins and outs of creating a successful business, you will likely spend years as well.

I developed my blog to help save people time by giving them the shortcuts they need to create a successful online business through trending digital marketing strategies.

After all, when trying to create and grow your online business you don't want to work all hours of the day, seven days a week. One of the most important things you can do when you build a business online is to get all the support you need.

Time is [money](#) and the faster you can get going the better!

Here are some ways to go about it:

Get a Professional Website

Before you launch your website to the world, it is very important to make sure it is the best it can possibly be. I can't stress this enough! You don't want to release a poor looking, unprofessional website that will leave your customers quickly dashing to someone else.

The web is a crowded ocean of competition and you must be able to stand out in your niche.

If you can get an honest critique of your website before you launch, you stand a greater chance of being successful with your online business. You could always launch your website and see how it does, but if it doesn't succeed, you have set yourself way back in time and dollars.

I'm not saying you need to spend $25,000 or even $5,000 on a website but it does need to be well optimized, easy to navigate and professional in appearance.

As you work to build a business online you need to look for credible help wherever you can so you can grow your business as quickly as possible. You don't want to take years to get your business to the point you want it to be.

With the help of experienced tactics, you can get the help and support you need so you can start seeing an active ROI (return on investment).

An Online Business Marketing System That Works

If you are interested in passive income and making money via affiliate marketing there is a system that exists that 100,000's of online marketing affiliates use and is believed to be the ultimate online money-making system.

This system which is called Wealthy Affiliate, worked years ago, works now, and will work for many years to come. It's a system that will show you just how huge the online world is and the limitless potential that only depends on what you are setting as your goal.

But before any money is generated, as I began, a proper website needs to be built, in your specific niche, and have a regular traffic flow of visitors.

The #1 attractor of visitors to your website is the quality of content on each page.

Short videos are also great to use on website pages. But until your website is built up with quality relevant content and drawing a flow of traffic, no money can be generated.

Once you build a solid foundation you can get to feel the thrill of making passive online sales.

There an empire can grow with a lot of consistent hard work (in the beginning), dedication, and great management.

There are said to be almost 4 billion people using the internet and with that great number comes with it a very large group of people who you can connect with and acquire great knowledge to go in any direction you choose to go.

Keep in mind, you don't want to take the advice of just anyone. Which is why I mentioned the community of Wealthy Affiliate. It's a good resource to get valuable information. And there's no cost to be in the group, and no purchase required.

Chapter VII

A Quick Look at How to Build a Business Online

The 4 Steps to get rolling:

Step #1 – Choose a niche. This can be anything and everything you can think of but something meaningful to you.

Choose a niche that you will enjoy of any interest, or passion, something that you are an expert at or even have no experience with at all but wish to.

If you're seeking how to hone in on a particular profitable niche, read my blog post; How to Choose a Profitable Niche for your Business.

Step #2 – Build up a website which is the foundation of your online real estate property.

First, your site must be built up and filled with information and content that visitors are searching for. It must be optimized for the internet correctly, mobile friendly, have a professional UX design and be easy to navigate.

Step # 3 – Draw traffic to your website, attract visitors that are interested in your niche. There are many ways to do this so it's best to start out with the free traffic options.

One basic strategy is to get traffic from organic searches, social media or YouTube [videos](#) in order to drive traffic back to your site or blog page. This then leads the viewer to a product offer or recommendation.

Article marketing or placing your website into related leading [directories](#) is a great way to enter a lot of content online for the search engines to rank, and for the viewers globally searching for that content.

Another strategy is to put one or more of the paid traffic options such as Facebook Ads, [Google Ads (PPC)](#) or Pinterest Ads to work to reach targeted groups of viewers from any niche and draw as many as possible into your funnel, or onto your website page.

Step # 4 – Earn Income – Once there is a traffic flow to the site you can start earning revenue.

There are multiple ways to [monetize a website](#) which I offer on my website for free and can give you unlimited earning potential.

#1 Recommendation: If you want to make money from your own online business, the first thing you need to do is promote it and promote it well.

Because like I always say, "If It's Not Read, It's Dead!"

Chapter VIII

Resources to Build Your Online Business

The Real Business of Blogging

Did you ever wonder how blogs make money exactly? Many people are curious in knowing how bloggers can earn anything from

$100.00 - $1,000,000.00 per month blogging. There are vast differences in profits and numerous ways that bloggers monetize their blogs. In fact, if you're a blogger, or considering blogging as a means of income, the secret is to never ever rely upon just one form of monetization.

This way, you always have another method to fall back on should one fall short. There are many profitable freelance services that you can offer on your blog or website. Some you can do yourself if you have the time and the talent, and some you can even outsource to others.

Here are some of the most popular and profitable ways bloggers make money:

- Affiliate marketing
- Advertising
- Sponsored posts
- Digital products
- **Offering products or** services

When you're just starting out as a new website and don't have much traffic, the best thing you can promote is your services.

The reason for this is because when you provide useful services you get to establish yourself as an **expert in your field.**

You build up your clientele, gain helpful testimonials, and word quickly spreads via social media and your inner circles that you are the 'go to' person to **call.**

This way your website or blog becomes your 24hr 'storefront' for your services and from there you can add other components of monetizing strategies to it! Such as affiliate marketing per say.

The Secret Sauce to Developing a Winning Business is YOU!

One of the best things about getting started with your online business is that previous experience is not a strict requirement. However, you need to be able to provide a service that will satisfy your customers and be willing to work hard in order to deliver the best quality you possibly can.

Your drive, passion, enthusiasm, creativity, persistence and motivation will eventually make all the difference.

People want to work with others who are passionate, enthusiastic and eager to do a good job.

The personal element truly plays a big factor when someone hires you or purchases from you.
There is a reason why they aren't hiring a faceless company: they want to deal with a person they can relate to, communicate with, share their ideas, thoughts and concerns with, and more importantly, develop a solid and long lasting relationship with.

Here are some examples of some successful online businesses to consider:

Start a Chatbot Business

The rise of the chatbot has been extraordinary to witness. Thanks to the ubiquity afforded to us by chat on platforms like Facebook, we've grown quite used to chatting with friends and family across all our social media networks.
That's why AI-powered chatbots present a new digital frontier for businesses looking to automate and relinquish much of the man-power it takes to have a chat with its customers.

This is abundantly clear when it comes to customer service. However, it's potent value in commerce has become quite obvious as well, and businesses across all spectrums are now taking advantage of this.

Platforms like Mobile Monkey, Manychat, ChattyPeople and several others have sprung up to take much of the confusion and complexities out of building a chatbot.

There's a proverbial gold rush happening today, of people trying to launch chatbots for their businesses to help automate some of their sales and marketing efforts that are needed to properly grow and scale in today's market.

However, similar to California's Gold Rush, those that will likely get rich are the ones that sell the picks and shovels. For that reason, why not launch your own chatbot business? Sure, there's some effort involved here, but this is definitely worth the steep learning curve.

Content Writing Services

Did you know that many bloggers have built up powerful online business by writing for others? If you already have a blog why not make some extra money by producing content for companies?

You can offer your brilliant eagle eye writing services to other industries and also offer web sales pages, proofreading, editing, or on page SEO or ghostwriting services.

If you are internet savvy, and enjoy reading then you have no doubt read, or contributed to various blogs. You probably have a few favorites that you keep up on, save in your feed and read on a regular basis.

You can make an unlimited amount of income by writing blogs and commenting on other blogs for various companies and websites which can turn into a full-fledged online business.

I know writers that have made upwards of 100K a year and who make $1,200+ in a single day of writing content for other companies. There's no reason why if you have a love of writing that you can't do the same. If you're not making the money you hope to be, you just may be going about it the wrong way.

Content and blog writing has become extraordinarily popular for internet businesses, film, television, radio and website owners in general. It is a way for people to interact with their customers or clients, for them to gain valuable information, and traffic, and get some much-needed feedback on how effective they are as a business owner.

The more people that comment and the more notice it gets the higher the website will rank in the search engines.

Businesses recognize this as an important SEO marketing strategy and is a very important aspect in terms of building their site's domain authority.

Blogs are a great way to keep customers informed of new products, sales items, industry news, education and more. Despite the sizable boom of video content in our faces these days there is still a tremendous need for quality written content across the board in thousands of industries.

Whether it's for social media, ads, news reports, articles, magazines, blog posts, brochures, websites, inspirational quotes, etc. there's a huge shortage of writers.

Companies are seeking content for everything from health/medical information to beauty and fashion to technical and finance, marketing, hospitality, relationship advice, travel, weight loss, pet care and more. The topics are pretty much endless!

Other businesses are more than happy to outsource it to a professional blog or content writer.

They will sometimes give you the subject, some keywords, and you can write and submit the blog or you can come up with them yourself. There are hundreds of topics you could write about, and thousands of blogs you could write.

Not only blog posts, there's other content that's needed and others are willing to pay for such as:

- Email templates
- Lead magnets
- Opt-ins

- Newsletters
- Social media campaigns
- Webinar scripts
- Templates
- Drip campaigns
- Landing pages
- White papers
- Blog topic ideas – the list is endless!

So, how can you get started building an online business with content marketing?

You can get started quickly and be on your way to building an online business and income with content writing. A quick search will net you hundreds of possible clients.

One of my first jobs was writing Instagram quotes for a California tee shirt company. They paid me $25 per 5 quotes! I was thrilled!

I prefer to write only about topics and subjects that I personally enjoy, otherwise it's drudgery and who wants that? I advise specializing in a particular niche that you know a lot about or one that you wish to become a master in.

Start with just a few at first, until you get more comfortable, and can take on more work. The last thing you want to do is get overwhelmed. Make sure that you can get all of your work in on time, before the deadlines.

Remember quality trumps quantity.

Copywriting Services

If you have a way with words you could freelance as a copywriter or content writer. Headlines are the gateway to articles and companies pay big bucks for people who have a knack to get other people to read their articles or emails. Good copywriting is key to the first step in making a sale.

Copywriters will always be in need in a variety of businesses. Bloggers, marketing and advertising agencies are seeking talented copywriters to write high converting sales pages, email campaigns, sales funnels, online ads, titles, and more.

If you want to hone your skill in copywriting, I highly recommend you get my course on how to create compelling copywriting for the web.

If you're going to start your own freelance writing business, as I mentioned it's vital you invest in a professional, polished [website.](#)

Your online presence showcases your services and represents you 24/7/365 so it's not wise to skimp on it to save costs.

I can't stress enough that if you're going to build your online business you must not go half way. Build your business with 100% of your energy and with the goal of making the type of income you want and need.

If you treat it as a fly by night hobby that you tend to whenever you feel like it will not succeed.

There is a lot of hard work in the beginning but once you get your procedures rolling a lot of it runs on auto-pilot.

I make an excellent living at this now but it took a lot of effort in the beginning.

It's also important to take the time to hone your skills, improve your craft and invest in yourself and what your clients are looking for, as well as staying on top of industry standards and the latest developments.

Aside from that you also have to remember that you will spend almost 80% of your time PROMOTING your business. This is key!

But the great thing about this type of business is you have the flexibility to control just how much work you wish to take on and how much you want your business to grow.

The better your skills, the more in demand you'll be. You will get to the point where you'll be able to pick and choose your clients, and eventually gain a reputation as a much sought out professional.

Whether you are a student, a stay at home mom, a retiree or you just want a second income, starting a business by producing high quality content writing or copywriting services is a fantastic option with unlimited opportunities.

Box subscription business

The box subscription business has exploded. While it's nothing new, and it's been around for ages now, the overwhelming rise of the internet has breathed newfound life into this online business idea.

What is a box subscription exactly? If you think back for a moment to one of the most viral box subscriptions businesses, you'll clearly recall the Dollar Shave Club.

Founded by Michael Dubin in 2011, the concept was ingenious in its use of a video that quickly went viral.

The company was sold for a billion dollars, and when you look at it from a sales funnel perspective, what Dubin did was brilliant. Like other box subscription businesses, there's a basic level of items that you can order.

Companies like Graze, Blue Apron, FabFitFun, beauty subscription boxes, Bark boxes for pets, and many others are on the rise.

In 2016, it was estimated by Shorr Packaging that there were 21.3 million box subscription websites, up from just 700,000 in 2013, a roughly 3,000 percent increase.

What's most interesting here are the consumer demographics. The typical visitor to a box subscription website makes roughly $78,436 a year and is in their early forties.

Graphic Design Services

If you have graphic design experience you have mad skills that will always be in fierce demand by many industries! Your website is a perfect place to showcase your best work and start a great online business!

Offer your Photoshop skills, images, Canva designs, or InDesign services for Pinterest pins, social media graphics, blog design, logos, guide covers, sales pages for entrepreneurs, businesses, bloggers, industries and more!

Photography Services

Thousands of businesses, bloggers and entrepreneurs are searching endlessly for styled stock photographs to use on their websites, in house and for social media.

If you have a DSLR camera, some decent props and a good eye maybe this is the online business you should start.

I feature several websites that offer millions of FREE styled stock photos that companies use regularly.

Many businesses also purchase a low priced subscription from various brands like Canva, Creative Market, Haute Stock, SmugMug and many others which makes the creative process that much easier and so much less time consuming.

You could specialize in a certain photography niche like cuisine, fashion, city-scapes, landscapes, floral designs, girl boss babes, nature, healthcare, children, travel, weddings, entertainment, or even a blend.

Ad management business

In today's highly-competitive marketplace, if you don't understand how to drive paid traffic and optimize your conversions, you need to turn to a company that does.

The truth is that paid ads can get incredibly complex.

Things like retargeting and custom audience definitions, along with understanding the ebb and flow of everything with a sales funnel, is complex and confusing to most.

However, if you do understand the mechanics of paid advertising, then you could easily launch an ad management business. Considering that ads are fueling the growth of tech giants like Facebook, Instagram, Google and YouTube, with loads of others coming into the mix, understanding and navigating the murky waters of paid advertising could position you to reap massive riches.

Why? Let's take a look at the numbers for a moment. Consider this: according to a report by eMarketer, digital ad spending in the U.S. will exceed traditional ad spending for the first time this year.

By 2023, digital will surpass two-thirds of total media spending. Total digital ad spending in the U.S. will grow 19% to $129.34 billion this year — 54.2% of estimated total U.S. ad spending.

The sheer facts point to continued explosive growth of online ads. And we're still in the infancy of the internet.

The earlier you capitalize on this industry, the quicker you can build it into a formidable online business. Study and learn all the intricacies of advertising on platforms like Facebook and Google.

Find courses, or use the free material available from a multitude of platforms to become a seasoned pro.

Web Design Services

Web design development and services are a hot business that you can offer for your online business. You should ideally be familiar with WordPress or Squarespace or another content management system, and have some experience with coding and knowledge of HTML and CSS as well as front and back end development.

However, in today's world you don't even necessarily have to know how to build a website from scratch.

I do believe it helps to be as knowledgeable about your craft for own benefit as well as your clients. However nowadays there are so many great drag and drop web builder programs like WebFlow, Weebly, Divi, Wix, Elementor, etc. that almost anyone can build a beautiful site without any html, java script, or coding knowledge. They've done it all for you.

With so many people on WordPress a lot of folks seek out help with WordPress. Some have even started online businesses specializing in exclusive help with Wordpress, so there's something else to consider.

SEO Business

Search engine optimization is a topic that I've been writing about for years now. The truth is that, while paid ads are growing at an astounding rate, the ability to appear organically and relevantly on search engines like Google is not only becoming more competitive, but also more lucrative.

When it comes to organic search keywords, there is sheer value at the top. Considering that roughly 40 percent of people click on the first search results and that the first page accounts for some 91 percent of the search share, appear organically at the top of Google's Search Engine Results Pages (SERPs) is something that is lusted and longed for by the world's foremost online marketers.

As the internet grows and expands, not only is SEO going to get more competitive, but it's also going to grow more lucrative.

There are big companies out there that pay up to $150K per month and more for quality SEO help.

You could quite easily capitalize on this industry if you know what you're doing. This doesn't just go for doing SEO work for clients, but also to improve your own website traffic.

You could launch any number of online businesses, niche websites, and blogs with the right amount of SEO skills.

Social Media Management Services

Even though there are a lot of automated social media programs out there like Hootsuite, SmarterQueue, Buffer, Tailwind, SemRush, Promo Republic, etc. businesses still need people to manage them.

Social media content consistently needs to be created in the form of tailored posts, video, answering posts, engaging, networking and growing with audiences.

If you enjoy working with social media platforms this could be a great online business for you to provide.

Social media managers make between $25-$75 per hour depending upon your demographic. As your own boss it's up to you to decide how many hours you want to work.

Being a freelance social media manager is a fantastic road to get started on making money from home in your spare time or full on gang busters.

Companies just don't have time to manage or keep up with all the aspects of social media's changing algorithms and requirements along with the demands of their own businesses.

Over 90% of marketers use social media to attract new business, but less than 15% are confident in their execution. Plus, they don't have the time to set up their social accounts and manage them properly! That has opened a huge market for those interested in starting their own social media businesses online.

Everyone from bloggers and entrepreneurs, start-ups to small, medium and large sized businesses and brands are looking for social media help.

On any given day a social media manager may be responsible for setting the strategy for an upcoming product launch, creating viral content, analyzing data, running paid advertisements and coordinating messaging with PR & communications. Basically being the voice for a company.

Many companies are desperately looking for help with social media and always will be. Digital engagement is only growing in popularity. Companies simply don't have the time to stay on top of all the newest changes and latest digital social developments and the latest algorithms sprouting up constantly.

They're too busy running the day to day operations of their own businesses.

This is where you come in. A social media agency is to be knowledgeable about all the different platforms that help business' grow; to be the liaison between brand and audience and help develop a loyal following, and be an engaging presence with the ultimate goal of turning viewers into longtime customers.

And, even better news, a formal degree is rarely required to be a social media manager or run a social media business from home.

Social media management is a very worthwhile career investment because it's something that you can get started doing with a very minimal investment.

Yet, you have the potential to make a fantastic return.

Because of the wide range of skills and tasks that a social media manager may employ, salary ranges from around $22,000 per year to over $115,000 per year – According to Salary.com

Being your own boss, the choice is really up to you how often you want to work, how many clients you wish to take on and what you will eventually earn.

Depending upon your financial and/or current working situation, whether you have young children or not, you may decide to work as a freelancer or even open up your own full-time business.

The opportunities are quite endless.

The other wonderful thing about being a social media manager is that you can literally do it from anywhere. Or, you can outsource others to do it for you and run the main aspects of it online.

And with advanced auto-posting capability nowadays, this can free you up to get more clients!

Very basically social media managers help businesses with managing their social media accounts, growing their online footprint and other types of social media marketing.

Most businesses see social media as a way to directly drive traffic to their website and force people to buy their products or use their services in pushy, salesy ways.

Social media managers know that this is wrong. There's a real strategy behind it.

They understand that real people use social media to build engagement with others.

Hence, they run marketing strategies that are focused on building positive relationships with these people.

Managers turn the spotlight on the 'social' in social media by creating & sharing content and asking & answering questions. This helps build a loyal fan base.

Businesses understand this.

Some more of the typical social media tasks companies want and you can offer your clients:

- Scheduling social media updates
- Sourcing viral content for sharing
- Community growth & outreach
- Responding to customer service issues
- Providing analytics (most social platforms have this built-in)
- Creating social media images
- Setting up profiles
- Providing optimal keywords
- Sharing popular posts and information on special offerings, discounts, seasonal events on a regular basis
- Paid advertising

With the right training you can start a successful social media management business from home in no time.

Creating Digital Courses

Another highly profitable online business that is growing like crazy presently, is creating your own digital courses.

These are usually created on a platform like Teachable or Udemy, or Podia which is what I use to create all of mine - These allow you to create beautiful, professional online courses for people all over the world with no technical knowledge or coding involved!

Online courses are a wonderful way to share your talents with the world and help other people get better at what they do too.

You know that tutorials and guides are huge on YouTube. But digital products and online courses make it simple to upload information like videos, pdfs, templates, files, and any other type of resource you can imagine.

If you want to know what the 12 most profitable digital products to sell online that generate hundreds of thousands of dollars each year for creators – read this post from my blog:

The 12 Most Profitable Digital Products to Sell Online

Selling digital products is also one of the best sources of passive income because a student can choose to take the course at any time and work through the course for as long as they like, thereby generating money for you **over the course of a lifetime.**

TIP! You know how I'm always stressing 'niches' - I highly recommend choosing to advertise your digital course expertise alongside a certain niche, for example Social Media for plastic surgeons, Sports car digital photography, Northern Italian culinary desserts, Excel for people who hate Excel, Calligraphy designs, How to Make 100K as an Affiliate Marketer, you get my meaning… rather than spreading yourself out too thin with a generic course. This way you can avoid having to compete in an area that is too overly saturated. You want to authenticate yourself as the expert in one specific area.

Digital products have many advantages that make them uniquely attractive to sell:

- Low overhead costs. You don't have to hold inventory or incur any shipping charges.
- Extremely high profit margins. There's no recurring cost of goods, so you retain the majority of your sales in profits.

- Potential to automate. Orders can be delivered instantly, letting you be relatively hands-off with fulfillment.
- Flexible products. You can offer free products to build your email list, monthly paid subscriptions for access to exclusive digital content, or licenses to use your digital products. You have a lot of options as to how you incorporate digital products into your business.

E-learning is the future of education. You have a massive opportunity to expand your business and impact with e-learning, an industry expected to be worth $331 billion by 2025.

In fact you don't even need a website to sell digital products! Of course, chances are if you do have a webpage or blog your sales are likely to increase.

You have the capability to send customers directly from your social media platform or an email to a sales description page, with a buy now button, sticker or link from Instagram.

There are numerous platforms, tools and apps you can use to sell all your digital products around the globe.

Affiliate Marketing

Affiliate marketing is one of my most favorite forms of monetizing my websites. I even wrote a whole guide on it which you can find in my blog Academy - it's called 'Mastering the Art of Affiliate Marketing':)

There are several affiliate marketers out there like Pat Flynn of Smart Passive Income and Michelle Schroeder Gardner who developed the popular course, 'Making Sense of Affiliate Marketing' who generate close to $150,000 per month from Affiliate marketing tactics.

Crazy right? They're not the only ones. The Penny Hoarder Blog, Youtubers, Instagrammers and more use affiliate strategies in their publications and social media posts and sometimes you don't even realize it.

Legally the FTC requires you to disclose affiliate links. But the point is that if you have a blog and want to monetize it, you can make an

excellent income once you know the correct strategies for affiliate marketing.

Affiliate marketing is the most profitable way to make money online.

Why I Love Affiliate Marketing

It's a great feeling to get up in the morning, turn on my computer, and see that I've made profits overnight. It's literally one of the best feelings ever!

And the best part is there's no limit to what you can earn, and from literally anywhere in the globe.

Affiliate marketing is a popular tactic to drive sales and generate significant online revenue.

Affiliate marketing is extremely beneficial to both brands and affiliate marketers, the new push towards less traditional marketing tactics has definitely paid off.

After all, passive income is a dream come true for most online marketers.

Here's how affiliate marketing works in a nutshell:

The idea behind affiliate marketing is that you have no product, but you don't have to create a product, and you never have to deal with customer service issues.

You promote a product that you feel will benefit your audience, fits your niche and you earn a piece of the profit for each sale.

It's a win/win for everyone involved. The customer gets the product or service they need, the company makes a sale and you make a commission.

These upstanding affiliate programs pay anywhere from 20%- 40% in commissions to partner with them. And they are companies in all types of various niches from healthcare to beauty, travel, fitness, business, design, household, culinary and much more!

These are highly reputable companies that are seeking quality bloggers to partner with them. You can not only earn some decent money by joining with them but your blog will grow in status for doing so.

With affiliate marketing you have the potential to generate a lot of passive income for a lifetime! As well as help your readers find products and services that you actually recommend and feel will be of value.

This is definitely something you don't want to skip over if you have a website intact.

Webinar business

I know what you're thinking. How do you start a webinar business? Well, webinars are quite possibly one of the best ways that you can sell anything online. The best part? You don't even need your own product.

Webinar guru, Jason Fladlien, co-founder of Rapid Crush, has grossed well north of $100 million in sales via webinars, which goes to show you the sheer power of this medium for selling.

Webinars offer an engaged audience that are ready and willing to purchase whatever it is that you're offering. As a fervent student of this medium, I've found explosive results await within a properly structured webinar. People like Liz Benny, Neil Patel and Russ Ruffino have been absolutely crushing it with webinars.

Either way you approach it -- whether you have an existing business or just want to sell as an affiliate -- some of the best webinar platforms that you could use in the world are GoToWebinar and Andy Jenkins' WebinarJam.

Virtual Assistant Online Business

Pinterest VA's are commanding 5 figure salaries helping bloggers and business owners manage Pinterest. Become an expert at this niche and start your own online business!

With over 6 million blogs out there and Pinterest being the main form of advertising to get traffic, it's no wonder!

How wonderful it would be to have a **Pinterest VA** to handle all the account management, designing of my pins, posting new pins, creating descriptions, optimizing, taking care of joining group boards, handling messages, managing and adding content to tribes, re-sharing, running analytic reports and scheduling of my pins!

I had a consultation with a few Pinterest entrepreneurs the other week and I was amazed to hear how much some of them were charging per month to manage Pinterest accounts. Upwards of $700-$2,000 monthly!

You don't even need a website to announce your services! Just create a detailed Facebook page, run a few ads and you're in business!

Coaching/Consulting/Auditing Services

Business coaching/consulting is a lucrative online business that taps into the massive market of online entrepreneurs and business owners who are trying to find their way into the world of online commerce.

If you're an expert in business or have an understanding of behind the scenes what drives purchases, then becoming a business coach could mean big money.

I notice that more and more bloggers are offering **coaching or auditing services** on their blogs. If you're a successful blogger and want to teach others I highly recommend this service. Certain bloggers charge $99 for a one on one personal strategy call or $799 per bundle session or more depending.

The best approach you can take is to offer an incredible amount of value upfront, and then have people pay you to execute it.

You can coach literally anything online now – there is a vast array of areas you can give advice on, granted you are an expert in the subject.

Some examples are; health and fitness, financial/budgeting, resume writing, relationships, spiritual, life coaching, organization, minimizing/decluttering, public relations, computer software, tax advice, and much more.

An example of a primary strategy for gaining clients and customers would be to analyze the business and understand where it is today, then discover where they actually want to be. Then figure out an approach to get them there.

Having a successful execution of a strategy is essential here. You want to instill confidence and you will need social proof. Grab some customers and offer them some free services to begin in exchange for testimonials. Then after they provide you with powerful reviews, position yourself to charge the higher ticketed rates.

Turn yourself into a global powerhouse by helping to consult, coach and deploy powerful strategies to draw in tens of millions of dollars from a [single funnel!](#)

Email Marketing Services

Email marketing is crucial for inbound sales. The money is after all 'in the list!" Companies pay entrepreneurs quite well to design and create emails for them. Email is 100x more powerful than social media.

Email is similar to copywriting in that you have to have the special ability to capture your reader's attention in the subject line so they actually want to click and open your email. Not always an easy task.

Many bloggers and business owners dread email marketing. There are **entrepreneurs** who specialize specifically in email marketing to take this task of busy business owners' hands by designing opt in forms, templates and landing pages to make their lives easier.

Some entrepreneurs exclusively make money designing email packages and **templates** for bloggers and/or business owners to purchase to save them the hassle of creating their own emails.

Branding Services

What's the difference between a brand and a business? Virtually nothing… But potentially everything. When building a business, whether you're aware of it or not, you're also building a brand. And everything you do, everything you say, everything you post and everyone you hire makes an active contribution towards that brand.

Many nascent small business owners can find themselves too caught up in the operational aspects of running their own business to give all that much thought to their brands. But fail to give branding its due consideration and you may find that your business fails to resonate with the people who make up your target audience.

A brand is the visual representation of your business. How else would we recognize top brands like Pepsi, Nike, McDonalds and other familiar brands?

It's all-too-common for new entrepreneurs to hire a freelancer to design a logo and come up with a fancy slogan and assume that these two things constitute their brand.

While both are undeniably important, they are just the tip of the iceberg as far as branding is concerned.

Your business is what you do, but your brand is who you are. It determines how you are seen by others both inside and outside of your organization.

Your brand should make a promise. It should represent a set of values that are directly tied to your mission statement. Your brand will leach into everything you do from how you train your employees to the tone of your marketing materials. It's in everything from the quality of your products and services to your customer complaints procedure.

Think about what you want people to feel or think about when they see your logo or hear the name of your business.

That's your brand. At least, it should be.

Remember that Consumers Do Judge Books by Their Covers!

We human beings are visually oriented creatures. It's how we learned which foods were safe to eat and which animals were most likely to try and eat us. Your brand can become a visual representation of your business and create positive associations among consumers.

Your branding can help consumers to attribute certain characteristics to your business and subtly influence how they perceive you.

If you're a blogger or creative, for instance, it may not matter how brilliant your writing, nor how elegant your graphic designs are if your website has an off-putting look or user interface.

Every business needs a brand. If you have a knack for pulling together colors, styles, looks, visuals you may be a true 'brander' at heart. Use your skills to your benefit to create a unique cohesive look for your clients and profitable service for yourself.

This is a fantastic online business service!!

Technical Services

Are you good at the technical stuff? Some, if not most people did not come with built in technical skills. I had to learn most of them on the fly while building my online business.

But if you are talented or experienced at WordPress, website development, installing themes or templates, or making or editing videos, imbedding code, deciphering analytics, performing SEO services, setting up an eCommerce store, then why not bank on those abilities?

This would be a very beneficial business and service to offer. I know many an entrepreneur who just want to focus on promotion and acquiring customers.

With everything a business owner has to do, they just don't have time to deal with the 'nitty gritty' technical stuff.

This is a very helpful line of business to be in.

eCommerce Shop

Speaking of eCommerce, another highly profitable niche you can cut your teeth on as an online business is the unparalleled power and diversity of eCommerce.

Many successful beginners work on the globally famous; Amazon, Shopify and Clickbank selling platforms and for good reason.

You don't have to have a lot of technical knowledge, they handle everything for you, and with drop shipping options and Amazon FBA, you don't have to store any product. Being a third party seller the beauty is, you don't have to deal with any customer service issues! It's pretty amazing.

With that being said, don't neglect doing your due diligence and homework before venturing full force into this highly intriguing platform with incredible potential as there are many different avenues to take.

Another great thing about these platforms is once you sign up they don't leave you stranded. They have plenty of continuing tutorials, guides and courses in their 'University' to help you on your way to be successful running your online shop.

These courses are extremely thorough and go through every last detail that you need to know to develop a profitable venture. Because after all, if you make money on their platform, so do they.

I highly recommend Amazon's FBA program.

The power of Amazon's dynamic platform and tools allow you to sell your own products and have them do all the heavy lifting!

The new Shopify integration with Amazon makes it even easier than ever to list and sell your products on the world's largest marketplace and get next-level brand visibility. With these two e-Commerce behemoths partnered together it's the ultimate time to get the store of your dreams up and running for major profits!

While your online store showcases your brand, and offers the most control over customer experience, expanding the ways you sell with Shopify allows you to do even more. For the right businesses, (you can use these folks to help you with your research here for locating all the top sellers) selling on Amazon can increase sales by reaching even more shoppers who are not already familiar with your company.

Benefits of Selling on Amazon with Shopify

If you're interested in expanding your business to Amazon, there are many benefits to selling using Shopify's sales channel:

- You can create new Amazon listings directly from Shopify in a number of categories
- For products that exist on Amazon, create offers directly from Shopify in any category
- Sync product details, variants and images to your Amazon Seller Central account
- Link Shopify products with your existing Amazon listings for any category
- Set unique price and reserve inventory just for Amazon listings

- Easily reconcile revenue from Amazon sales using Shopify reports
- Sync inventory tracked by Shopify with Amazon listings
- Fulfill Amazon orders directly from Shopify

There's no limit to what you can sell on Amazon or Shopify as an entrepreneur either part or full time!

The hardest part will be doing the research into deciding what you want to sell and what niche is most profitable. Check out my blog posts on Amazon FBA to get started in this lucrative online business.

What Online Business Will You Start?

These are just some of the many, many online businesses you as an online entrepreneur can start.

Important! Keep in mind there are some **very important** things to know when starting your online business that we'll get into below that can actually make or break your chances for success.

Read on for tips to get the most out of your online business.

Chapter IX

Top 10 Secrets to Success When Starting Your Online Business

So how WILL you become successful with your online business? I mean after all you're not doing this just to make ends meet and 'get by' right? You are in this to earn some big profits I would imagine.

I know, you're thinking that starting your own business and working on your own terms and on your own time is very enticing. It brings a sense of freedom and independence, and many people are eager to experience the ability to follow a career they are actually passionate about.

Having said that, your practical side knows that becoming a **full-time business owner and entrepreneur** that makes that kind of money is not something that happens overnight.

You need a plan which is exactly why you're super smart to have done your homework and purchased this guide.

Success as an entrepreneur can be a long and steep road. The good news? You can get there quicker if you seek to offer real value, and really put your mind and more importantly ACTION to it.

These are my TOP 10+ Secrets to Becoming a Successful 6 Figure Entrepreneur

1) Focus on a Specific Niche, and Excel at it.

Notice how I keep stressing Niches? This is #1 for a good reason.

One of the biggest mistakes in the entrepreneurial world is thinking that you can do everything.

"I may not know the road to success, but the road to certain failure is trying to please everyone". I forget who said this but it's certainly true.

Even if you do have multiple talents, and we all do, look at it this way: would you rather eat a meal at an amazing restaurant known for a small, yet enticing selection of succulent and unique mouth-watering dishes, or would you rather eat at a nondescript run of the mill establishment, with a huge menu filled with subpar choices?

Customers expect a "boutique" experience from an entrepreneur running an online business.

Instead of trying to do everything, focus on a limited amount of services in a **niche** you are really good at. This is the best way to start building a solid reputation for yourself.

2) Get organized.

Being an independent full-time entrepreneur requires a ton of **discipline**. You won't have a boss breathing down your neck no, but you will have deadlines so you will have to be responsible for the quality and timeliness of your own work.

Being disorganized and completing tasks at the last minute means that you will likely experience a lot of issues, and deal with very dissatisfied customers which will cost you money.

Learn the importance of being focused, organized and start marking your to-dos and daily tasks in your calendar!

Don't do this and you will pay the price and suffer from being in total chaos and have some really pissed off clients.

3) Avoid 'Shiny Object Syndrome'

Shiny Ball or Shiny Object Syndrome can be an absolute killer for entrepreneurs and business owners of all types. As a solopreneur I mentioned one has to be laser focused on one's tasks and projects. It is absolutely vital if you're going to survive in this atmosphere of endless fancy side trackers.

Every day there are new distractions, enticing emails, lurking around the bend that are being launched, thrown in our faces and newbie entrepreneurs and marketers are being lured from their main objectives causing us to go in different directions.

Here's a tip!

When working turn off all electronic objects. The phone, the computer, social media, everything. Ok, maybe some commercial free music in the background.

There's just too many distractions and temptations out there to pull you away from your work.

The end result is that nothing will ever get accomplished. Not only that, while you're in hot pursuit of the next shiny object countless amounts of time and money is wasted along the way without thought as to whether this new service, product or idea is truly a good investment for your business.

As an entrepreneur the only 'shiny object' you need to invest in really is yourself and what will next make your business succeed.

Here are some remedies to avoid the disorder of 'Shiny object syndrome'.

Think of it like going to the grocery store when you're hungry. You don't need the cherry cheesecake but you want it. But is it truly necessary? What purpose will it serve? Will it truly benefit you, or will it just fill out your jeans more, empty your wallet and ultimately make you unhappy.

4) Document all your ideas

Note down every tool that tempts you. When something new catches your attention, put it in Evernote or in a Word doc and then right away return to whatever you were doing before.

The problem with these ideas is that we think they suddenly are top priority and because of that they need to be implemented straight away and therefore need your full attention.

Writing them down means you can stop worrying about them and review them later on in the day.

There are two methods to try and help reduce the distraction, one is to set aside sometime in the day to brainstorm new ideas. The second is to have a weekly plan of activities, this way you can focus on your current tasks without being distracted.

5) Take a "Pause" Before Starting Anything

This is one of those things that I have to remember as well. When an idea pops into your head, pause.

Don't do it straight away. It doesn't matter whether the idea is just doing some tweets or redoing your keywords - both ideas can wait.

Setting some time aside to consider your concept and if you should implement it. If after your designated time you still think the idea is good and will help your business, then make plans to execute it.

Otherwise leave it alone and don't fret about it.

If you find you really need it, it will come back to you.

6) Have a Long-Term Business Strategy

Now that you have a list of ideas, it is time to weigh up whether they are genuinely worth consideration.

In order to do this, you have to look at them in the context of your long term strategy and ask the question "Does this idea align with my business goals?" - will it put me on the fast track towards where I need to be or can I outsource it to someone else?

If the answer is yes, then proceed. If not, then put it back into the bucket and revisit it later on. Or by all means outsource it.

Some of your ideas may need other things to be accomplished before they themselves can be implemented.

For the time being if something really is urgent, try outsourcing the task, that way you can continue working towards your business targets.

7) Stay Focused on Your Mission with a Positive Mindset

The following is all about the importance of mindset as an online business owner. I believe it's crucial for anyone starting a new business to master the correct mindset first and foremost before anything else.

After all:

Your Mindset Will Determine Your Success

We've all heard the expression by Henry Ford

"Whether you think you can, or you think you can't you're right".

No truer words have ever been spoken.

It's all about mindset. And as an entrepreneur, independent solopreneur, business owner - you'd better have only one thought - that you absolutely can.

In fact, yes you CAN. There's absolutely no reason you can't. You're going to mess up. You're going to fail at some things. A lot of things. And everybody does.

But not at everything.

Once you make a decision, the universe conspires to make it happen. Ralph Waldo Emerson

Creating A New Mindset

As an entrepreneur there are going to be days that seem to take so much effort just to get through and others that seem to pass without a hitch?

What is it that makes the difference in our outcomes?

One word sums it up: **Your Mindset.**

Outlook, attitude, perspective, preparation, and beliefs play a large part in forming our mindset. Our current mindset was formed from our outlook on life, attitudes, perspectives, preparation and beliefs.

Our mindset is influenced by our prior experiences and how we evaluate them, our definition of self and our assumptions about current or new situations.

Our level of awareness determines how well we can consciously filter out the internal thoughts and the external messages which work against what we hope to achieve and allows our mindset to expand.

"Sometimes later or in a minute; becomes never, do it NOW".

Creating a new mindset begins with seeing a new situation in relation to our past experiences and contrasting that view with the current quality of life we experience.

As humans we are programmed to do what **we are comfortable** doing. When faced with a new choice, we automatically compare what we assume the new experience will be to our prior experiences.

We learn wisdom from failure much more than from success. We often discover what will do, by finding out what will not do; and probably he who never made a mistake never made a discovery. – According to Samuel Sales

Consciously Choosing Your Mindset as an Entrepreneur

When you woke up this morning what was the first thing you thought about? Or rather, what was your attitude?

I remember that sweet older guy in the movie Jerry Maguire who clapped his hands every morning and said "It's going to be a great day today!"

That's the mindset you have to have. Whether or not it turns out to be true it makes a difference in your **whole attitude.**

"We tend to live up to our expectations". Earl Nightingale

When I used to focus on my competition and thought about how wonderful other people's blogs were compared to mine, all that did was **paralyze my efforts** and cause me fear and confusion if what I was doing was even worth it. Absolutely nothing good came of it.

Instead I decided to focus on only me and what I was doing and needed to get done.

Where you focus your attention is completely up to you. You have the power and control.

You cannot control how others react to you. Only how you react to others and yourself.

Sure, you'll make mistakes and do silly things at times where you'll say, "What was I thinking?" But it's important to realize we're only human.

Don't sabotage your efforts by qualifying what you say

Use more **powerful** words to describe something you want to accomplish by replacing these words or phrases (or others like them): try, have to, doubt, can't, never, take forever, too hard, don't want, think, maybe.

It's important when in business for yourself that you feel confident inside to accomplish what you set out to do. You can 'fake it til you make it', but you won't make it for long. You must truly feel it. Helping your words will help to change your mindset.

Do you see what's wrong with the following sentences? Are you guilty of using this language?

- The only experience I have to offer is from a long time ago.
- I am not really good at this yet.
- I might make some money at this
- I'll try to find out.
- I guess so

- I am not sure if I can attend.
- It's not like I intend to hurt anyone; I just say it like it is.
- I just never have been able to stay organized.
- I plan to be famous one day.
- I wish I had more time.
- I meant to follow up; I just haven't yet.
- I have been so busy I haven't been able to get anything done.
- I usually pay attention to detail.

The ability to reword these statements indicates that you are beginning to develop a new mindset.

Continuously catch and correct yourself if you find yourself slipping backwards.

Remember, just like a gardener who sows seeds, you have to tend to the new mindset in order for it to flourish.

8) Learn The Power of Customer Service

One of the most fundamental aspects of starting an online business is the ability to deal with your clientele. It's important to remain helpful, courteous and communicative in any situation, and go the extra mile to keep an open line of contact with your customers before, during, and after each project.

Your customers are the **lifeblood** of your businesses, and if you don't take care of them, they might look elsewhere for other options!

The harsh reality of being an entrepreneur is that you are going to be a drop of water in a small ocean. There are many competitors out there, and the one key element to succeed over others is to develop **killer customer service ethics.** This will make you stand out and be remembered.

People nowadays are more than impatient, myself included. I remember one time waiting and waiting for another writer to get back to me. She kept saying she just had to get back to her desk top. After several hours she finally wrote back and said, 'sorry, I had something to do'. So did I. I hired someone else! Not professional at all.

Responding as rapidly as possible to your inquiries is crucial these days. If you don't do it they will go elsewhere. It's super easy in this day of technology. We all get busy but a friendly I'll be with you as soon as I can goes a long way. Acknowledgement is very important.

More importantly, **don't lose your cool** if you are dealing with difficult customers. Be polite and helpful and refrain from responding to abusive behavior by arguing or being condescending to your customers. Even if you think you did a good job, you can't convince an unsatisfied customer to like your work and be happy.

The truth is that even the best entrepreneurs have unhappy customers, and you simply need to learn how to deal with it without escalating the situation to a time-consuming and potentially dangerous personal conflict. Your reputation will be largely defined by how you treat your customers, in both good and bad situations. Consistent customer service is a huge skill that you will definitely learn to perfect overtime.

Go above and beyond.

In addition to great customer service, you can also stand out by going above and beyond. Your customer needs the finished work in 4 days? Deliver it in 3. You got paid to write 200 words? Write 300. While you shouldn't feel obligated to do extra work, going **the extra mile** and throwing in some extras can be an amazing way to win over the hearts of your customers and turn them into returning clients. Having said that, watch out for customers who take advantage of your generosity!

Work out the Kinks in Advance.

Before accepting money and getting started on a project, take some extra time to really work out the kinks with your customers and discuss the project in advance. Some entrepreneurs want to get to a sale as quickly as possible, but this is actually an easy gateway to problems and misunderstandings.

On the other hand, discussing with your customers and working out the details of the project in advance is an easy solution to prevent claims or other issues, and to **set the boundaries** of a project very clearly.

9) Know When to Say No

As a new online business many entrepreneurs love to take on as many projects as they can, especially if they are just starting out. However, it is important to know when to say no. If a customer has realistic expectations or if you have a feeling that they'll give you a hard time, the best solution is to respectfully decline to work with them.

As a beginner, it might be hard to say no when you are hungry for new work, but remember that quality is more important than quantity. A bad customer or project that will leave you feeling too overwhelmed can be a huge loss in terms of money, energy and time, 3 assets you are going to need badly, especially at the beginning of your career.

Don't let greed make you accept a project you don't think you do the absolute best on. In the end it will wind up backfiring on you.

Be clear and upfront about important project details.

As mentioned earlier, it is important to discuss with customers prior to getting started with a project. This includes establishing clear conditions concerning the project's deliverables.

Pre-determine how much you want to get paid and the amount of work to be done, to make sure that you won't experience any claims or other issues. Keep track of all the conditions ahead of the projects, and meticulously store everything in your archives.

As an entrepreneur part of being organized is also keeping records not only for your clients but also for yourself. You must be able to retrieve whatever items you need in case you ever need them to 'cya' or cover your a** if the need arises.

10) Invest in yourself.

As an entrepreneur, you are essentially starting a business, and like most businesses, you will need **promotion**. You should not skimp on investing in yourself, because this is how you can improve your career and reputation. Invest money in good branding, advertising, or even specific education and certificates that can make you stand out from the crowd.

Many people fail to realize that this is a very important step. Promotion is almost 80% of business. You can't just create an account on a freelance platform and expect the money to roll in. ***Be active and truly work for yourself.*** This is your career, and you should be able to understand the importance of professional growth. As the old saying goes, you have to spend money if you want to make money.

Don't be a wallflower when it comes to promoting yourself and your skills. You must be bold about it and get the word out there now that you are a business owner.

Otherwise, how will others ever know about what you have to offer?

Collaborate with others and befriend fellow entrepreneurs.

Many entrepreneurs tend to work alone. However, teaming up with other entrepreneurs can be absolutely amazing, especially if you aren't directly competing with them.

For instance, if you are a back end web developer, it might be useful to network with talented front end developers or graphic designers.

This is another example of how you could upsell your services if you were an 'affiliate' for a company you liked. The company would make a sale, you'd make a commission and your reader would get a fantastic product that they needed. A win-win for all.

In the case of recommending another entrepreneur to your customer you could even up-sell your services as a package, with the collaboration of your freelance "colleagues" and you could both make a profit. There's many different scenarios you could benefit from partnering up with another entrepreneur.

Even without directly teaming up with another entrepreneur, if you refer them to your customers, they might be really thankful, and in turn, refer you to their own clients. As they say, "If you scratch my back, I scratch yours!" Supporting each other can be absolutely essential for entrepreneurs. This also includes sharing resources, suggestions and ideas.

The article below is by expert blogger Ryan Biddulph who lives in Thailand working as a digital nomad and talks about the importance of promoting other bloggers even though he is a top blogger himself! He doesn't see it as competition. Other bloggers help him to raise his popularity rate and in turn he does the same. No man is an island as they say!

More Tips for Success!

Learn to up-sell

Entrepreneurs can make a lot more money and significantly increase their bottom line if they learn how to up-sell their customers correctly. Are you a blogger? You don't have to limit yourself to simple article writing.

Offer extra services such as SEO-optimization, text analytics, social media consulting, alternative headline options, design services and so on.

Additional services that you can attach to your core offering are a little bit like the candy near the checkout counter at your local grocery shop: it's an impulse buy trigger, and it allows the shop to **make more sales!**

Providing added services to your customers also means that you can be considered as a **one-stop solution** to the needs of your buyers.

Let's face it, as an entrepreneur sometimes you can't and shouldn't do everything yourself.

Chapter X

How To Get Paid as An Entrepreneur

If you are starting your online business or work through a freelance platform, you should only accept payments according to the specific rules, methods or guidelines allowed by whichever platform you're working through.

When you do not work with a specific freelance platform, the risk of not getting paid can be somewhat higher.

Having said that, there are many ways to protect yourself.

One of the most common ways to protect your work from dishonest customers is to require advance payment.

You can ask for a certain amount of money in advance in order to get the project started.

Many entrepreneurs usually ask for half the fee upfront, but your mileage may vary. Some entrepreneurs only require <u>20%</u> or <u>30%</u> of the total cost to be paid in advance.

On the other hand, others prefer to get paid in full before getting started with the order. It is really all about what works best for you and for your particular line of services.

The best way to protect yourself is by having [legal templates](#) or contracts and agreements in place beforehand.

It is very important for both you and your customers to feel comfortable with any transaction. For this reason, you should also learn more about the power of flexibility.

If you think you and your buyer can meet half way when discussing the financial aspects of the project, do so. Be always open to negotiations and further communication.

While it is always a good idea to cater to customers and entice them with discounts and other incentives, you don't want to sell yourself too short.

If you think that a potential customer is trying to lowball you a little too much, you should take it as a big red flag. Customers who are trying too hard to get unrealistic rates are usually difficult to work with in many other ways. For this reason, they might simply not be worth your time.

Dealing with difficult and unpleasant customers can actually put a lot of strain on your workflow. It can slow down other projects and put a damper on your overall mood and motivation. It might sound counter-intuitive, but you should be selective on your projects.

One of the best things about being an entrepreneur is that you get to pick your battles and work on projects that you are passionate about!

At times, "No" is the right thing to say, and you should never be afraid to use this word.

Every single time you say "no" to a project, you might be choking up inside, and you might feel like you are missing out on a new opportunity.

However, some projects are doomed from the start, and pursuing them is simply not worth the trouble you're probably going to have to go through to fulfill the customer's demands.

If you are in doubt about a specific project or customer, always follow your senses. If you have a gut instinct that's telling you to stay away, you might be better off by listening to your sixth sense, after all!

Before accepting a new project, you should also consider what else is already on your plate. Don't take on more work than you can realistically handle. Otherwise, you might just end up with not one, but a string of disappointed customers!

As a beginner, it is very tempting to give in to absurdly low-paying jobs. While this might sound like a good idea to get started, my advice is to avoid doing too much work for very little in return.

Don't give in to promises of visibility and more work in the future. When a professional relationship starts on such uneven ground, it is almost always a bad sign. Be patient and be good at what you do. You will definitely have the opportunity to shine and work with a reputable customer.

Chapter XI

Highlight Your Experience

As mentioned earlier, you do not need to have any previous professional experience when you start your online business. However, if you do have any experience, make sure that you take advantage of it. Highlight your background and make it count, without boasting too much about it.

There is always a fine line between sharing your accomplishments and turning your self-presentation into a boring resume! Keep reading to learn more about presenting yourself and adding value to your experience.

When you provide services online, you need to be able to prove yourself to your customers. Your background matters. This is why you should have clear work samples and a portfolio at hand. These elements are absolutely essential to give your potential clients a better outlook on what you're capable of. This is where the power of self-presentation kicks in.

You should always have a small biography, detailing who you are, what you do and what your background is. Aim for something small and compact. You want something that potential customers can read very quickly, and come out with a good impression. Here is an example:

"John Smith is a copywriter with over 20 years of experience. He has worked with major national brands and magazines, including XXX, YYY, and MMM.
John has a passion for sharing powerful stories and empowering brands with great content"

The text above is roughly 40 words in length, and it is written in the 3rd person perspective. This format is deemed easier to read, and it gives the text a nice professional touch. Notice how the first line of the bio immediately states some very important information:

"John Smith is a copywriter with over 20 years of experience."

With just a small sentence, we're able to convey some key information. We're giving away the name of the entrepreneur, the area of expertise, as well as the amount of professional experience.

Later, the bio goes on to mention some notable clients, to give further credibility and legitimacy to the entrepreneur's work. This is a very sensitive step and many people get it wrong. You don't want to write a grocery list! Even if you have worked with dozens or hundreds of customers, stick to just a few for your introductory buy. Don't mention more than 3-4 names.

The final paragraph of the bio has a more personal and "human" connotation. It is about showing off your passion and your professional motivation. Why should your customers pick you? Why are you the right person? Because you aren't just performing a task. You are doing something that you're passionate about.

Many entrepreneurs took a big risk quitting their jobs and pursuing an independent career on their own. In most cases, it would never be possible without the right passion and dedication. This should come through your story, and you should use it to connect with people!

Organize your portfolio

Now that you have a nice short bio, you need to pair it up with some portfolio samples.

When creating a professional portfolio, it is very important to keep it relatively compact. You don't want to overwhelm your customers with things to check out. Instead, create an "anthology" of some of your best work. Picks 4-5 examples for every category of services you provide and make sure that you organize them properly.

For example, if you are a photographer, make sure that you organize your gallery in such a way that your clients can easily navigate various services.
Don't mix your portraits with product shots or landscapes! Have it all organized and ready to go, so you can actually direct clients to specific sample categories.

A well-organized portfolio will also make you look more professional and trustworthy, so it is a really good idea to spend some time to get it right!

The Importance of a Business S.W.O.T. Analysis.

Many new companies and start-ups take the time to do a S.W.O.T. analysis before "putting all their eggs in one basket."

S.W.O.T. stands for "Strengths, Weaknesses, Opportunities, and Threats." These are some of the most important aspects to consider when you build your business from the ground up, and this also goes for an entrepreneur.

Strengths:

Understand the value of your strengths and figure out how you can highlight the best qualities of your businesses. What makes you special? What makes your products/services stand out?

Weaknesses:

Every business has weaknesses. What are yours? It is very important to understand your weaknesses and find ways to overcome them or play around them.

Opportunities:

Any good business should have enough room to move forward. Define your opportunities and come up with ways to grow professionally. Figure out ways to expand your services. Come up with ideas to upsell your customers, and create ongoing relationships with your clients.

For an entrepreneur, each interaction is an opportunity. Value every person who contacts you. It is essential to build relationships with fellow entrepreneurs to extend your professional networks.

Threats:

You should consider anything that might threaten your income and the long-term viability of your business. For instance, audio engineers need to consider the looming and constant threat of automation.

Today, artists can get their music publicized almost instantly and for very little money, using automated online software and on social platforms like [Tik Tok](#).

How will this affect your pricing? How will you compete in the market? It's important to evaluate present and future threats in order to come up with a viable business plan and service structure that will keep you afloat from years to come.

It is also important to be able to adapt to sudden changes in the market. This way, you will be able to immediately respond to unexpected threats and change your business model accordingly.

Chapter XII

Be prepared to invest some money in your online business success.

Most start-ups and businesses need a starting investment capital in order to get off the ground.

Many entrepreneurs think that they can start off without any investment whatsoever. On the other hand, investing something into your business can be the difference between succeeding and failing.

Investing in your business is investing in you. As they say, you have to spend money to make money!

It's not realistic to expect to sit in front of a laptop, create an account on a freelance platform and wait for the sales to roll right in.

Here's some things you will need to invest in to grow your business:

Invest in Better Equipment

You wouldn't find a ballerina with worn out pointe shoes or a newly hired sous Chef with sub par cooking gear. Investing in better equipment will enhance your online business.

Sure you may think you can work with the latest version of Adobe and last year's SEO software but is your competitor? You'll be falling behind.

There are many self-appointed experts or self-styled jack-of-all-trade types out there. The problem with these entrepreneurs is that they claim they can do everything, but they aren't really excellent at anything.

Don't be that type of entrepreneur. Instead, be someone who's highly specialized in your niche, and be absolutely top notch at what you do!

Talent and skills are very important. However, equipment is also important. Having better professional equipment related to your specific industry will make it easier to produce better work.

In addition to that, owning good professional equipment will actually make you look more credible in the eyes of your customers.

For example, if you are a photographer working with a great top-of-the-line camera, you'll certainly be more impressive on paper than someone who works with a consumer-grade DSLR.

Again, I'm not saying that you have to have expensive equipment to be successful.

However, if this is your life's work then investing money in top-of-the-line equipment that does the job will put you ahead.

Keep in mind - Decent equipment can also be a good tax write-off, and a justified expense to enhance your business.

Starting out as a copywriter/content creator I did not technically require any specialized equipment in order to write.

However, I still decided to invest some money on a decent computer/laptop, a good workspace and decent software. A nice desk and a good chair make for a comfortable environment, preventing posture issues and back/neck pain.

My little working nook also keeps my motivation higher, and having a dedicated workspace helps with separating my professional life with other areas of my daily life.
Regardless of what your area of expertise is, there are always ways to enhance your daily workflow and invest in your success, even if it simply means purchasing a more comfortable office chair!

Spend money on promoting your business

There are many ways to promote yourself as an entrepreneur. You can put in time and effort to market yourself through social media. You can also use blog posts and other content creation tools as a way to expand your audience and spread the word about what you do.

Having said that, spending money on promoting yourself can be an excellent way to further raise your profile.

Advertising your work on social media platforms can be an incredible way to build more traffic. In particular, this is a useful thing to do ahead of sensible business periods. For example, many entrepreneurs are quite busy in the months before Christmas.

Many companies hire entrepreneurs to maximize their content before their busiest sales period. You should take advantage of the opportunity and invest some money in promotion ahead of the busy season.

You might find that you can easily improve the way you reach out to customers, and even a relatively small investment in online ads can significantly boost your sales.

If you aim to appeal to local businesses, you can consider advertising on local media such as magazines, newspapers and local websites.

Appealing to local clients can be an amazing way to strengthen your ties with the local community, and ads are often a great way to spread the word about your business.

It is always a good idea to allocate a yearly budget for advertising, even though most entrepreneurs actually neglect this practice.

The key is to start looking at yourself as an actual small business owner: why wouldn't you invest in visibility? You aren't just throwing money out the window.

You are actually expanding your reach, and the newfound visibility can lead you to sales and hopefully, lasting relationships with new customers.

Chapter XIII
Why Better Branding is Essential

Many entrepreneurs vastly underestimate the importance of a great brand. There is nothing shadier than visiting an entrepreneur's website, only to find out that their photos are some outdated cellular phone selfies, and their logos are bulky, corny fonts that were probably put together by someone who knew nothing about your business!

Your brand is who you are, and you want people to get the best first impression. This is the reason why you should invest money into your personal brand.

Hire a photographer to take some professional portraits of you. Great photos that show off your image and professionalism are absolutely essential.

A good, professional photo shoot will make you stand out from those entrepreneurs that use downloaded images, emojis or worse, pictures that have been taken with their phones.

The thing I recommend doing if you want to offer more for your services is creating a one – five page website that markets your services and highlights your best work.

These [websites](#) are simple to make. You can even outsource it to another entrepreneur and have it done in less than a few days! There are also templates out there if you are creative and wish to pick it out yourself that are designed to simplify the process even more.

When you create your website make certain that you have lead generation in mind and a definite call to action. The purpose of your site after all is to generate more clients.

This is what makes your business survive and thrive! The more leads you have the better chance you have of getting sales and building up your reputation.

In addition to that, you should consider hiring an experienced designer to bring your website and social media pages back to life.

Get a great logo, and reference some of your best competitors to see what they're doing right. Don't copy them, but get some ideas from their style, so you understand what customers are responding to in this particular industry.

Generally speaking, avoid messy designs and opt for a minimalistic approach. When possible, slow down with stock images and choose to hire a photographer to create images ad hoc for you.

Whether you need a new logo or a good picture, don't skimp on branding. This is a relatively small expense given the number of talented entrepreneurs working in this industry. In addition to that, a really good logo can last you many years before you need to update it!

It is important to understand that spending a ton of money on your business is not a requirement. You don't need to invest any money at all if you want to be a successful entrepreneur. Some people actually start from a position of financial instability, and they simply cannot afford to invest any money as they begin their career. However, investing in your development can really make a huge difference in your professional future.

Even if you cannot afford to spend money right away, you should consider investing in the development of your personal brand and business later down the line, as you start earning some money as an entrepreneur.

Another idea is to create a powerful 'landing page' also called a squeeze page. This is created to entice people to want to learn more about what you're offering with a form to fill out for more information.

Once the page is created, let your audience know that they will receive a FREE option or gift for signing up.

This is called an 'opt in' or 'lead magnet'.

This is an excellent way to create your master email list which is the ideal way to get in touch with your target audience or people who you know are definitely interested in what you have to offer in the future.

Chapter XIV

The Essential Tool of Email

Maybe you've heard the term 'The Money is in the List'. I cannot stress enough how vital an email list is to your success having an online business.
It hands down CRUSHES social media and other forms of promotion.

Email is a hugely powerful and **essential tool** for everyday online business. As a beginner blogger or online business owner you absolutely need to have an effective email campaign.

'A 10,000 email list is worth $100,000 a year in business'. – According to Blog Tyrant.

Repeat after me, social media alone won't cut it. In fact, Email *is proven to beat* social media for converting people into long term customers.

Yes, I know we are all bombarded with email in our inboxes from companies we don't want to hear from and we wonder how the heck did we get on that list?

But I don't want to send emails you say! Marketing firms spend thousands on talented copywriters to develop catchy subject lines just to get potential customers to open emails. What are the chances that your email is even seen or will it wind up in the junk bin? And why do you as a new entrepreneur, blogger or website owner even need an email campaign?

Why The Heck Do I Need an Email List?

- You have direct access to your readers.
- You increase sales every time you share an amazing offer or product.
- You get better ideas and feedback from readers.
- You get great personal connections you can't accomplish using social media.
- You get help and support when you need it in the form of feedback from your readers which in turn helps you to help them, which helps you and so on and so forth...get my drift?
- You grow expertise by helping your readers one on one.

1. Create Emails people will want to open

It takes awesome email content and subject lines to create interest, pique interest and to stay interested in your emails and therefore your online business

Just like any relationship in your life, your potential customer, reader, buyer needs a reason to stay connected to YOU, a purpose that YOU are giving to them that only YOU specifically, and no one else can fulfill. Your content plays a major role here.

The acronym WIIFM (What's in it for me?) is VITAL in your customer becoming a long term subscriber!

2. Sign Up for Email Marketing Software

When I first started blogging I read from other bloggers to not wait to sign up for an email marketing service but I was hesitant because I didn't have anything to offer. Now I totally get it and I'm reiterating their message here to YOU about why it's so important – Do not wait another second to sign up for an email service such as ConvertKit. It's vital to the success of your online business that you do!

- **Email is Personal** – Email allows you to land into a user's inbox. There is no ranking system limiting your reach. It is very direct, personal, and casual.
- **Email is Purposeful** – To get your email a user needs to sign up for your email list and confirm their email address. Someone doing this much work is obviously interested in hearing from you, and they are much more receptive to your message.
- **Email is Targeted** – As we mentioned earlier the user has already shown interest in your products / content. Since you already know what they like, you can deliver them highly relevant content and offers to get better results. This is called segmentation, and we will cover that later in the article.
- **You Own Your Email List** – You do not own Facebook, Twitter, or Google. Your social media campaigns and SEO efforts can go to waste when these platforms change their policies. On the other hand, you own your email list, and it is not influenced by decisions of other businesses.
- **Email is One-on-One** – People read email in the privacy of their inbox. The message is not on a public timeline or newsfeed. They can ask you questions directly in private with confidence. This helps build trust and connection.

This is precisely why every smart business in the world has an email list. To grow their online business and capture more subscribers who visit their site.

3. Offer a Free Giveaway in your email:

In your email you can run an online contest and offer free giveaways, an eBook, a digital download-able product, a free printable, a pdf, a course, a planner, or any type of other valuable resource that you feel matches up with your niche for your reader.

Adding a bonus of your own can help convert followers into purchasers. If they are getting a great deal, then it would be quite hard for them to turn down the offer. Sometimes people make a purchase either out of curiosity or just because the bonus is that great!

4. How to Create an Engaging Opt-In Message:

Use these 5 proven ways to create an engaging **opt-in message**.

1. **Use Social Proof** – or a 'Herd Mentality' – If it's good enough for 1,000+ people it must be good enough for me! i.e. 'Join 8,000 followers on Twitter and subscribe to our list'
2. **Humanize the Benefit** – Touch on 'pain points' that your audience has. Answer questions that potential readers have that you can possibly answer for them.
3. **Make them feel Exclusive** – People like to feel like they're on the 'inside' of something – offer exclusive access to privy info.

4. **Offer an Incentive** – If offering a product, try Free shipping or a discount.
5. **Are They Worth it?** – You're the expert and they want what you have – offer access to your hacks and expertise in exchange for their email.

5. Use Your Facebook Page for email signups:

Facebook is the major platform for online marketing, promoting your offers & making money online. It's also a tremendous way to build your email list.

You can post your online business services on the timeline of your Facebook page. It's preferable to do this on your FB business page rather than your personal page in my opinion. But every now and then it doesn't hurt to throw in a business post on your personal page.

Don't forget to always add a call to action button or email sign-up form FB page too, so if there are any new product launches or services, you can easily share them on your Facebook page and add your website link and email address so people can easily check out your business.

Chapter XV:

Advanced Customer Service Lessons

Managing ratings and dealing with grouchy customers

As discussed earlier many new businesses out there work on freelance platforms such as Fiverr **or Upwork but there are many others.**

One of the main aspects of dealing with your clients through these websites is to learn how to manage your businesses' ratings.

They can also help you interact with customers in the most professional way. Regardless of whether they decide to leave a positive or negative rating, don't underestimate the importance of interacting with your clients as professionally as you can.

Positive ratings are extremely important. As a seller, you should strive to do your best to do quality work, and go above and beyond to please your customers (without, of course, letting them be abusive of your time and hard work).

Having said that, it is important to understand that you simply cannot please everyone. Sooner or later, you will receive a negative review. This happens to the best businesses out there.

If you visit any review websites or consumer opinion aggregator, you will notice that even the most beloved companies out there have at least some negative reviews.

One of the biggest mistakes entrepreneurs make is that they go to great lengths to suppress negative reviews or attack their customers. This is not an appropriate response. Keep reading to learn more about how to deal with negative ratings, the right way.

Thoroughly Consider the Buyer's Negative Ratings.

If you receive a negative rating, you shouldn't immediately write it off thinking that you're right and the customer is wrong. Instead, you should ask yourself questions.

Does your customer have a point with their rating? Is there really something that you can improve with your service? Many entrepreneurs are blind to negative comments, thinking that if someone has a problem with their work, well, it's their problem!

This is a very destructive attitude for your business because it means that you aren't open to understanding your faults and growing as a professional in your field.

Are you receiving negative feedback constantly? Are you struggling with too many bad ratings? In my experience, this is not the customer's fault. If you find yourself dealing with more than the occasional negative rating, perhaps you need to seriously consider the feedback you are receiving and take the opportunity to improve your ways.

Say Thank You:

Whether you receive a negative or positive rating, it is always a good idea to reach out to your customers and say thank you. When I receive a positive rating, I usually send a message to the buyer, telling them how grateful I was and that I certainly hope to work with them again soon.

On the other hand, I tend to write something positive to customers who weren't happy with the work either. Not all negative ratings are abusive. Some people might simply not like your work.

As a writer, this is something I often deal with. At times, my writing style simply does not match the personal taste of the buyer, and in spite of offering revisions, it's quite hard to please someone who already made up your mind before you even started the work!

When I receive negative or lukewarm ratings from people like that, I don't take it personally. I write them a note that reads pretty much like the following

"Hi there, thank you for taking the time to leave a rating and sorry that the content I provided didn't work out for you - All the best with your project!"

By being nice, you can turn situations around. Instead of acting angry, I reply politely with a message similar to the one I posted above.

Believe it or not, some unhappy customers actually came back to me, probably after trying other sellers that didn't leave a good impression) and the second time around we actually worked something out for the better!

Be open to communication and discussion

If you have a problem with a buyer's rating. Don't get angry and don't become too emotional. Even when it sounds like buyers are being rude, abusive or condescending, keep your cool.

Most buyers might act aggressively, and lose their temper over a tiny problem, or a small request that was misunderstood.

In some cases, they simply might not understand that communicating with a seller is the best way to solve problems, instead of barking and threatening.

Well, being the understanding one is your job! When a customer is aggressive towards you, don't fight back. Be polite, stay positive and offer ongoing support. If someone insults you, do not insult back, in any way. Instead, always remain calm, answer politely and record everything.

If things fall down the drain, you can always contact customer service representatives (if you work on a freelance platform) or if push comes to show, collect material for legal action.

In most cases, the tension between you and a difficult customer can simply be avoided by not feeding the flame with more heat! It's important to understand that in our society, customers are "educated" in very peculiar ways.

Throughout the past few decades, overzealous salesmen have established that "customer is always right" mentality, which really went on to define how most modern customers see themselves.

No, the customers are not always right, but they think they are, and there is nothing that you can do or say that will change their minds! This is the reason why arguing with them is pointless. Absolutely pointless, like screaming against the waves crashing on a shoreline to shut the heck up.

Don't Argue: Communicate!

Go as far as you are willing to go to please your customer. Be open to revisions, additional work (within reason) and more.

If you feel like your buyer has been taking too much of your time, abusing your willingness to find a solution, put a stop to it.

When you think you already did everything you could do to try to make it better, you can put a stop to the situation by simply saying

"I am sorry to hear my work wasn't to your satisfaction. I've provided as much additional assistance, revisions, and support. You are welcome to purchase additional work/revisions at a discounted fee, or you can choose to close the project and leave any rating you see fit - thanks again for your time!"

This is often a worst-case scenario and it seldom comes to this, but you need to know when to stop.

You can't juggle around nagging customers like a trained monkey, or they will drain all your time and energy that you would otherwise need to process the many other projects in your queue!

Chapter XVI:

The Importance of Marketing Your Online Business

One of your biggest responsibilities as a successful entrepreneur is to market yourself the right way.

If you neglect marketing, you'll likely end up losing a lot of significant exposure and good traffic.

Even if you think you've been doing pretty well without any marketing, think about what you could actually achieve if you decided to put some real effort into self-promotion!

As an independent entrepreneur, you are probably already quite busy as it is.
How in the world will you ever find the time to market yourself, if you have deadlines, orders, customers to deal with and other obligations?

The answer is simple. Make time and be prepared to work a little harder until you get your automation systems in place.

Many companies can afford to hire consultants or in-house crews that are essentially always focused on marketing.

As an independent entrepreneur, this might not be a viable option for you. For this reason, you need to reap the benefit of working smarter. Learn to run the show as a one-man/woman-band!

Top Social Media Platforms for Promotion

The most natural approach to marketing is to try to appeal to people across various media. Most experts will tell you to create an account on every social media platform, and post content every day, everywhere. This strategy might work for a company, but as a solo endeavor, you might struggle to take care of so many media outlets.

The other thing is not all social platforms may be best suited for your type of business.

The best approach is to limit yourself, so you can actually focus on creating quality marketing content on selected platforms, rather than disseminating uninspiring promotional material everywhere.

Pick 3-4 different platforms that you feel really comfortable with, to begin with. In particular, focus on those social media websites that would better suit your line of work.

Are you a photographer? Use Instagram and Tumblr to showcase your work. Are you a writer? Create a personal blog and share some of your best articles!

Do you work with videography? Vimeo and Animoto are excellent programs to create professional videos.

If I had to pick only 4 platforms to promote myself, I'd stick to Facebook, Instagram, Twitter, and Pinterest. I'll explain why I believe that these platforms are actually really incredible for entrepreneurs to market their services, regardless of their professional niche.

Facebook

Facebook might not be the most exciting social media platform out there, but it is somewhat of a default for most people. You can rest assured that some customers might at least try to look you up on Facebook for inquiries or information.

Maintaining a page on Facebook is a relatively low-effort endeavor, and it is a really good place to list important contact details, share news, engage with your customers and build a solid network.

Instagram

What I really love about Instagram is the immediacy of this platform. You can write captions, but what really matters is the power of visual content. You can easily use this powerful platform to build a following and post relatable content every single day.

The possibilities are endless, and you can also use it to your advantage to build better relationships with your customers.

Imagine you're a graphic designer who just created a new logo for a company. With the permission of your customer, you could upload a photo of the logo, with some nice hashtags (#) to promote your content and show off your skills. In addition to that, you can tag your customer as well.

Most of your clients will love this because they can benefit from extra exposure for their brand, and they might be keen on reposting your content as well, thus giving you some visibility in return. It's a win-win situation!

Instagram is also a really good place to interact with like-minded entrepreneurs everywhere. If you are interested in logo design, look up for all the posts filed under #logodesign.

Check out some pictures, like them, comment on them, and start conversations with people. This is a nice, organic way to grow your traffic on Instagram and get your name out there.

I like to give myself at least 10 minutes a day where I just focus on my Instagram promotion, posting new content, as well as checking out my feed, commenting on pictures and joining discussions on other people's feeds.

Warning: don't overdo it! If you send blanket messages out to everyone, you might damage your image and come off as a visibility leech. Avoid corny copy-paste comments like "Wow, great content! Come check out my photos as well."

The best approach is to simply comment on something you're interested in, and offer something genuine to the conversation.

Twitter

I have a love/hate relationship with Twitter. On one hand, it's quite hard to grow organic followers unless you are a celebrity and post tons of content every day.

On the other hand, it is a good place to expose your work, promote your freelance business and interact with others in your network. Twitter isn't hard to manage. Try to do at least a post a day!

Pinterest

Pinterest is hands down the best platform for bloggers, growing exponentially with over 200 million viewers a day. It has a ton of helpful features, and more importantly, it is cleverly optimized for mobile users.

I love to use the "carousel" and 'story' features to promote multiple pins at once, and send the links out to my customers whenever they ask to see samples of my work.

You can also create various group boards on your account which is a great way to build your following.

This way, you can easily showcase different aspects of your work to different viewers.

Tumblr

Tumblr is another great platform to appeal to people, particularly through cool images, videos and more. You don't even have to spend a lot of time creating new content: re-post anything that you think might be interesting to your customers and that somehow might relate to what you do!

LinkedIn

LinkedIn is a MUST for businesses to get more exposure and network with one another. It's a great place to engage with others in your niche, share your work and even present your portfolio.

The Ultimate Ways to Promote Your Business

It seems as though every day there are more digital promotional tools being developed.
On my blog I've created a huge number of posts on how to utilize social media technology to the fullest, as well as a jam packed list of over 100 ways to promote your online business, products or services all in one handy place.

It's perfect not only for bloggers but for anyone in the digital scope hoping to drive more engagement and traffic.

Chapter XVII

More Tips for a Winning Online Business

Keep bringing value to your customers.

Many entrepreneurs underestimate the importance of networking with their previous customers. Once you make a sale and process an order, it doesn't have to end there. You should still bring value to your customers.

There are many ways to go about it. For instance, follow your customers on social media. I love to keep up with their feed and participate in their achievements.

To give you an example, I recently worked on some product packaging for a company. After months of development and hiring various entrepreneurs, they finally managed to launch their product on the market.

As soon as I learned about the company's product release, I immediately retweeted the news, offered my congratulations and wrote a small post about the company via Twitter.

"Congrats @Vintageconfections for the release of your new lollipops! They look so scrumptious. #newlollipops #customlollipops #confections"

Needless to say, the company was delighted about the post. As a small firm, it makes them look really good that someone is actually writing about them.

For this reason, they actually retweeted the content (Notice how I didn't even ask them to) and they gave me some exposure in return.

With such a simple and effortless gesture, you can easily build better relationships with your existing customers, as well as extend the range of your visibility…and all you need to do is…be nice!

Ad Campaigns

It might be a good idea to invest in ad campaigns a couple of times a year.

In my experience, September and October tend to be the busiest months of the year. This is because a lot of people prepare their products and their marketing for the Holiday season.

During these times, many businesses hire entrepreneurs like me to make sure they are prepared for their busiest period!

For this reason, it wouldn't hurt to invest in online ads ahead of such a busy time for entrepreneurs. If you advertise your services just before a time that is particularly busy for your industry, you might be able to find a bigger audience and further expand your reach, attracting businesses seeking for the type of services that you can provide.

Online Facebook Ad campaigns run from affordable to expensive but can easily fit into any small budget.

They can be strategized to run specifically during certain dates and for particular demographics targeted by age, location, interests, etc.

Google Adwords PPC campaigns are another option.

The benefit of them is that you can advertise your services and you only pay when someone actually clicks on your ad.

Focusing on keywords is important and be certain to target the areas only where you would like to work.

You can work globally or locally online. This is a great way to muster up quick business because you don't have to wait for organic SEO to kick in. Your ad shows up immediately.

Chapter XVIII:

Life-Work Balance When You Have an Online Business

Life-Work balance is one of the most overlooked and misunderstood aspects of being an entrepreneur. As I touched upon in the beginning of this guide, we all hear about those fairytale stories: being an entrepreneur is awesome! You're free to work wherever you want, you can travel, you have no boss...and so on.

All of the above perks are absolutely based in reality.
It is really amazing to be able to work anywhere, anytime and on your own terms.

Even as I am writing this page, I am sitting in an outdoor amazing little Italian restaurant right next to the glorious intracoastal in South Florida listening to live music.

I don't have office hours, and I can work for as long, or as little, as I want to every single day.

Having said that, you shouldn't just assume that this lifestyle is a walk in the park. Being an entrepreneur means that the more you are willing to work, the more you can earn and grow professionally. In the beginning however, you may find yourself working far more than some of your friends with 'regular' 9 to 6 jobs.

I must admit it's hard for me to have my own 'off' button at times.

Here are some important tips to stay in the game.

Avoid Burn Out

Working for someone else you can disconnect. As an entrepreneur, solo-preneur, independent contractor, freelancer having your own business you often need or get used to working around the clock.

Managing emails, answering messages, dealing with customers across multiple time zones, and other commitments.
This routine wasn't easy to adjust to in the beginning. During the first few years, I've actually struggled with the sheer amount of never-

ending work. I'd be checking my inbox in the middle of the night, and sure enough, there would be many new messages to reply to.

I'd be working from the early hours of the morning to the late hours of the evening, with short breaks in between.

It did not take very long for me to suffer from a good case of burn-out and realize that this was not good for me, on a personal and professional level.

As an entrepreneur, it is not immediately easy to separate your work and personal life, because there are no set boundaries.

Creating such healthy boundaries is very important and absolutely vital in order to maintain a sustainable long term career and keep up the quality of work that people begin to expect from you.

For myself, I went from working 12-16 hours a day, to working 5-8 hours a day. I was convinced that I was going to lose a lot of business working fewer hours, but I also thought that I simply needed to face that risk because my mental and physical wellbeing needed to come first.

However, the results actually surprised me.

I soon realized that although I was working half the hours I used to work earlier, I actually worked faster, and better. I had a lot more energy, and I looked forward to completing tasks as quickly and as efficiently as possible. I became more productive, and my business became all the more successful for it.

Why work so hard if you can't reap the benefits of your hard work as an entrepreneur? Today, I value my free time, and I realized that relaxing, pursuing my hobbies and simply taking my mind off work for a few hours really makes me work better. My usual day consists of waking up early in the morning (usually at 7 or 8 AM) and then depending on the day sometimes until 2 or some days until 6, depending.

In my opinion, this is a very healthy way to work as an entrepreneur, because you can put in a really decent number of hours, and it doesn't feel like it.

For me, getting started earlier means that you can take advantage of the rest of the day, and truly make every moment count!

This method works for me, but it's important for you to find the chemistry and balance that suits your life and routine! Just remember one thing: don't become a slave of your online business.

Use it to empower yourself and live the lifestyle you want to live!

Taking care of yourself

When you work for a company, you can probably expect many benefits (although perhaps nowadays it's more a thing of the past) – such as health insurance, dental, paid leaves, 401K, and other benefits.

Such benefits have often been a distant dream for most entrepreneurs. Having said that, things are changing for the better.

Today, there are many companies that are actually focusing on providing health insurance plants for entrepreneurs.

Many of the leading freelance platforms out there, including [Fiverr](#), are actually teaming up with various insurance providers in a bid to offer entrepreneurs viable health coverage plans.

Many younger people who just started out as entrepreneurs might not think too much about these particular aspects of their career and lives.

For this reason, they actually might end up regretting it later down the line.

Health insurance for example, is important especially if you have children, and if something ever happens to you, and you don't have enough funds to cover your medical expenses, you could get in serious trouble.

Since the Coronavirus pandemic I put together a list of small business resources from various sites on my blog to help small businesses around the country.

Chapter XIX

Final observations

Hopefully, this guide gave you some interesting ideas and resources to tackle your online business head on!

I want to use this closing space to wish you all the best with your entrepreneurial endeavors.

Please don't give up if you don't see immediate results. Becoming established can take quite some time, so you can't expect to explode overnight but once the work starts flowing, it literally can take a swift turn and you can get very busy suddenly so it's important to pace yourself and pick your projects wisely!

Many entrepreneurs usually start by being able to make a nice side income, which eventually turns into a steady full-time revenue stream! It's very much what you put into it. Just remember, you want to work 'smarter, not harder'.

It is important to understand that there isn't a single one-size-fits all formula. You can't write a perfect recipe for success as an entrepreneur.

There are simply too many variables involved. The industry you focus on, your characteristics as an individual, your particular situation in life…the list could simply go on forever.

Making it as an entrepreneur is ultimately your own path.

This guide will hopefully enlighten you and give you some ideas.

Remember that it is completely up to you to determine what will really work best for you in your particular scenario!

The most important thing is to stay focused, dedicated and consistent, and to pick a niche you're passionate about.

Use the right tools, be certain to take the time to promote yourself, and learn how to deal with your customers. This is how you will succeed as an online business entrepreneur!

Thank you so much for all your support!

www.ingramcontent.com/pod-product-compliance
Lightning Source LLC
Chambersburg PA
CBHW062107220526
45471CB00010B/3629